Leopold Zunz, Perets ben Barukh Asher Perles

Hebrew Characteristics

Miscellaneous papers from the German

Leopold Zunz, Perets ben Barukh Asher Perles

Hebrew Characteristics
Miscellaneous papers from the German

ISBN/EAN: 9783337316495

Printed in Europe, USA, Canada, Australia, Japan

Cover: Foto ©ninafisch / pixelio.de

More available books at **www.hansebooks.com**

HEBREW

CHARACTERISTICS:

MISCELLANEOUS PAPERS

FROM THE GERMAN.

ולתעודה.   כתורה

NEW YORK:

American Jewish Publication Society.

October, 1875.

PREFACE.

The translation of the following essays being prepared for the general reader rather than the student of that branch of Jewish literature to which they belong, it has been thought advisable to issue them in their present form unencumbered by the purely literary and scientific ground work of the originals. The names of their authors may be accepted as a sufficient guarantee for the correctness of every statement contained in them. In the translation, the competent reader will recognize the hand of a master of both idioms, and acknowledge that it is as faithful and polished a rendering of the original as the difference of idioms permits.

PUBLICATION COMMITTEE
of the A. J. P. S.

Table of Contents.

—

EXTRACTS

FROM

JEWISH MORALISTS.

Eleventh to Fifteenth Century.

FROM

Dr. ZUNZ'S

"Zur Geschichte und Literatur."

Extracts from Jewish Moralists.

ELEVENTH TO FIFTEENTH CENTURY.

From Dr. ZUNZ'S "Zur Geschichte und Literatur."

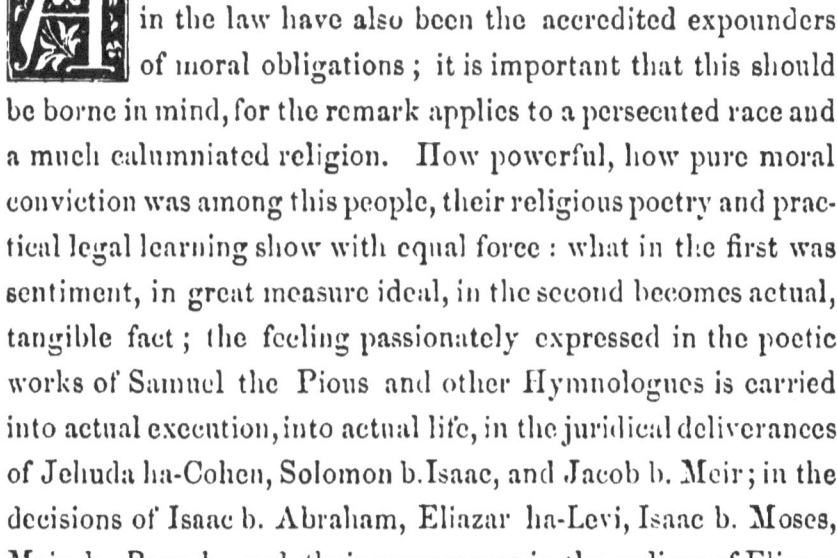

AMONG Jews, investigators of texts and men learned in the law have also been the accredited expounders of moral obligations ; it is important that this should be borne in mind, for the remark applies to a persecuted race and a much calumniated religion. How powerful, how pure moral conviction was among this people, their religious poetry and practical legal learning show with equal force : what in the first was sentiment, in great measure ideal, in the second becomes actual, tangible fact ; the feeling passionately expressed in the poetic works of Samuel the Pious and other Hymnologues is carried into actual execution, into actual life, in the juridical deliverances of Jehuda ha-Cohen, Solomon b. Isaac, and Jacob b. Meir ; in the decisions of Isaac b. Abraham, Eliazar ha-Levi, Isaac b. Moses, Meir b. Baruch, and their successors ; in the codices of Eliazar of Metz and Moses of Coucy. But the teachers of that age were not content with the working on the minds of the educated, and the learned in the Halacha, they sought themselves to mould minds to appreciate moral distinctions, to appreciate essential morality by oral discourses in the Synagogue, by special ethical treatises, by original exposition and treatment of religious subjects. When, some seventy years ago, a Professor cast a casual glance on one of these writings, he exclaimed with condescending approval, "In such times as those we could hardly expect to find even from Christians such moral teachings as this Jew (R. Asher in Toledo) inculcated upon and transmitted to his co-religionists." But the truth is, that the ethical doctrine of these Jews need not blush in the presence of any of later origin; and the Israelites of the German middle age, children of the devil as they were, stand immeasurably higher in the moral scale than the Priests of Tyrol of two hundred years ago, for example, among whom gluttony, laziness, unchastity, stupidity, and heathenish superstition were almost universally to be found.*

This ethical literature is composed partly of interpretative notes on the old Mishna Abot, partly belongs to exegetical or halachic works, either as suitable comments upon special passages of the earlier books of exegesis or as separate treatises. Sometimes they have the form of testaments to children and family connections; sometimes they have allegorical or poetical form; sometimes they are direct exhortations to lead a moral and God-fearing life. Between the years 1050 and 1490, at least thirty works of this sort might be specially named. Let us listen to the very words of some of these old teachers. They will amply repay attention.

* Beda Weber: "Tyrol und die Reformation." Innsbruck, 1841.

R. Eliezer b. Isaac (about 1050).

From Orchot Chayim.

My son, give God all honor and the gratitude which is his due; for He it is who made thee and brought thee into this world. Thou hast need of Him, but He needs thee not. Put no trust in thy mere corporeal well-doing here below! Many a one hath laid him down to sleep at nightfall, but at morn risen not again; many a one hath gone to his couch at nightfall sound in health and of high cheerfulness, and has waked up to agonies and terrors. Fear the Lord, the God of thy fathers; fail never at eventide to pronounce the great word wherein Israel is wont to proclaim that He is, and that He is One, and One only; at dawn fail never to read the appointed prayers; see that thou guard well thy soul's holiness; let the thoughts of thy heart be saintly when thou liest waking in the bed, and profane not thy soul, even in the hour of most intimate communing with others, with words of impurity. Be thou cleanly in things that concern the body; wash well thine hands ere the morning be far gone; and when thou seest that they are clean and pure, fold them then in prayer. Praise thy Creator when thou puttest on thy clothing, and when thou takest the nourishment that supports life. Be among the first to reach the house of God; enter it with reverential awe. Think well before whom it is thou standest there. When thou goest to the place where the law and the truth are studied, let no idle word pass thy lips; note well in mind the words of the sages there; deem not that anything there is small and of slight account, and beware that thou never allow thyself to look down on any one. Visit the sick and suffering man, and let thy countenance be cheerful when he sees it, but not so that thou oppress the helpless one with gaiety. Comfort those that are in grief; let piety where thou seest it affect thee even to tears; and then it may be that thou wilt be spared the grief of weeping over the death of thy children. Respect the poor man by gifts whose hand he knows not of; and when he eats at thy table gaze not on him too much, lest he doubt his welcome; be not deaf to his beseechings, deal not hard words out to him, and give him of thy richest food when he sits at meal with thee. When thou prayest, be lowly and think thyself nothing before the Almighty, and use all thy soul's energy and force to hold in check what evil desire there may be in thine heart. Greet every man pleasantly, speak truth only, forget not modesty, and in thy eating be moderate; rather feed thyself with the vilest weed than make thyself dependent on other human beings; and seek not greedily after power and pre-eminence in the world. From a wicked neighbor, from a person of ill fame, see that thou keep aloof, and spend not much of thy time among people who speak ill of their brotherman; be not as the fly that is always seeking sick and wounded places; and tell not of the faults and failings of those about thee. Take no one to wife unworthy to be thy life's partner, and keep thy sons close to the study of divine things. Dare not to rejoice when thine enemy comes to the ground; but give him food when he hungers; be on thy guard lest thou give pain ever to the widow and the orphan; beware lest thou ever set thyself up to be both witness and judge against another; and when thou passest judgment, see that thou invoke counsel from another mind. Never enter thy house with abrupt and startling step, and bear not thyself so that those who dwell under thy roof feel dread when in thy presence. Purge thy soul of angry passion, that inheritance of fools; love wise men, and strive to know more and more of the works and the ways of thy Creator. Forget not that the hope of pious souls is that concealed paradise prepared by God before the foundations of the world; that consecrated place where pure spirits and holy enter at last into their rest.

R. ELEAZAR B. JEHUDA OF WORMS. (OBT. 1238.)

From Rokeach.

No crown carries such royalty with it as doth humility; no monument gives such glory as an unsullied name; no worldly gain can equal that which comes from observing God's laws; the highest sacrifice is a broken and contrite heart; the highest wisdom is that which is found in the law; the noblest of all ornaments is modesty; the most beautiful of all the things man can do is to forgive wrong. Cherish a good heart when thou findest it in any one; hate, for thou mayest hate it, the haughtiness of the overbearing man, and keep the boaster at a distance. There is no skill or cleverness to be compared to that which avoids temptation; there is no force, no strength that can equal piety. All honor to him who thinks continually and with an anxious heart of his Maker; who prays, reads, learns, and all these with a passionate yearning for his Maker's grace. Such a one bears about with him unrepiningly the burden of his nation's faith, holds worldly delights in contempt, is moderate in all the workings of his mind, is master of his passions, and, in sooth, has God continually before his eyes. The path which his feet tread is straightforward, and the words which he utters to others are soft and sweet; he educates his children for a worthy life, infuses love and righteousness into all his works, seeks to lead others into the right way; he reverences his wife and is inflexible in fidelity to her; he sees that his children take to themselves husbands and wives as soon as may be, after age fits them for wedlock; is of a contented mind, and rejoices when the world goes well with other men. Such a one loves his neighbors and friends, lends to the needy, gives alms secretly, and does good purely and simply for God's sake; such a one you will find early and find late in the house of study and prayer, where he may add to the store of his knowledge and may pray from the depths of his reverent heart. God's blessing be on him and on his children.

Do not inquire too curiously concerning thy Creator, or seek by mere questioning to know the origin of things; but see that God is never far from thy thoughts; forget not what He has done for thee, and let not strange gods, let not thine own sensuous nature hold dominion over thy life. Let thy dealings be of such sort that a blush need never visit thy cheek; be sternly dumb to the voice of passion; commit no sin, saying to thyself that thou wilt repent and make atonement at a later time. Let no oath ever pass thy lips; play not the haughty aristocrat in thine heart; follow not the desire of the eyes, banish carefully all guile from thy soul, all unseemly self-assertion from thy bearing and thy temper. Speak never mere empty words; enter into strife with no man; place no reliance on men of mocking lips; wrangle not with evil men; cherish no too fixed good opinion of thyself, but lend thine ear to remonstrance and reproof. Be not weakly pleased at demonstration of honor; strive not anxiously for distinction; never let a thought of envy of those who do grave wrong cross thy.

mind; be never enviously jealous of others, or too eager for money. Honor thy parents; make peace whenever thou canst among people, lead them gently into the good path; place thy trust in, give thy company to, those who fear their God. If the means of thy support in life be measured out scantily to thee, remember that thou hast to be thankful and grateful even for the mere privilege to breathe, and that thou must take up that suffering as a test of thy piety and a preparation for better things. But if worldly wealth be lent to thee, exalt not thyself above thy poor brother; for both of ye came naked into the world, and both of ye will surely have to sleep at last together in the dust.

Thirteen passages in the Pentateuch enjoin upon us the love of God; and when the temper of a man is filled with love for his God, he needs must serve his Maker faithfully, though men should seek to drag him from the service by main force. For then man is filled as with a consuming desire to mould his life according to God's will, and delight in God makes us forget all the world's delights. He who is possessed by the love of God sets not the store he did on the raptures of his wife's, the delights of his children's love. For nothing can be the real business of his life save to fulfill divine commands, to see that God's name is recognized as holy, to bring to God the sacrifice of his undivided life. Men of this sort do not exalt themselves above others, indulge in no idle talk, long not wretchedly for the love in woman's eyes, are silent when blame is poured on them; for their thoughts are not where they are themselves, but ever with Him whose praises are sung by their faithful lips.

Let the man of humble mind carefully evade all marks of special esteem and recognition from men. If his failings are spoken of, let him give God thanks for putting this humiliation on him for the amendment of his ways, if they need it. But if he is well and surely convinced that they need it not in that wherein they blame, let him after all remember that whatsoever he be, he is but imperfect compared with what is required of him, and forgive the person who is speaking ill of him. Wholly incompatible with a humble spirit is loud and passionate talk, falsehood, uttering of oaths, mockery, unrestrained desire, vengefulness; the humble man seeks not revenge for injuring treatment, but bears it with unruffled temper; if calamity strike him, if his property be taken from him, if he lose children or near relations, he does but acknowledge devoutly that Providence is just. When his conscience tells him that he has offended against his brother-man, he confesses the wrong, and he does not too eagerly confute and confound one who has spread abroad falsehood concerning him. My son, shake off all haughtiness of mind and cling to humility, cease to exalt thyself in thine own estimation, and be of lowly mind and temper; let none of thy failings appear small or trifling in thine own eyes, but all of them weighty and great; remember whence thou camest and whither thou goest; repent, atone, and serve thy Maker with love; free thyself from passion and desire before thy light is quenched, before thy soul is required of thee, before the book of thy deeds is opened for judgment.

The thoughts of thy heart and the imaginations of thy soul remain pure if the work of thy hands be pure. Fly from all unseemly things; close thine eyes, thy ears to them with stern decision; for there be desires which cause the soul to be apostate from God. Therefore in the days when thou art still young, think of Him who made thee, of the heavenly Father

who supported thee, clothed thee, and requite him not ungrate-
ful by delivering up thy soul to impurity. Bear well thy
heart against the assaults of envy which kills even sooner than
death itself; and know no envy at all, save such envy of the
merits of virtuous men as shall lead thee to emulate the beauty
of their lives. Surrender not thyself a slave to hate, that ruin
of all the heart's good resolves, that destroyer of the very
savor of food, of our sleep, of all reverence in our souls. Keep
peace both within the city and without, for it goes well with all
those who are counselors of peace; be wholly sincere; mislead
no one by prevarications, by words smoother than intention, as
little as by direct falsehood. Would ye know why men die
before their time? It is because they lie. For God the Eternal
is a God of Truth; it is He from whom truth flowed first, He
who begat truth and sent it into creation. Let the fear of God
breed in thee the habit of silence, for much speech can hardly
be without some sin. But when thou dost speak, speak truth
only, speak never praise of thyself, and speak ever moderate
thought in modest words.

If thou hadst lived in the dread days of martyrdom, and the
peoples had fallen on thee to force thee to apostatize from thy
faith, thou wouldst surely, as did so many, have given thy life
in its defense. Well then; fight now the fight laid on thee in
the better days, the fight with evil desire; fight and conquer,
and seek for allies in this warfare of your soul, seek them in the
fear of God and the study of his law. Forget not that God
recompenses according to the measure wherewith ye withstand
the evil in your heart. Be a man in thy youth; but if thou
wert then defeated in the struggle, return, return at last to God,
however old thou mayest be, and even in the later years thou

2

wilt find healing and safety in His hands. Sin not in secret, and be not ashamed to fulfill the commandments of God in the sight of men; reckon up aright, make no foolish mistake as to what thou owest to God, what to man. Murmur not because the world goes well with the powerful and wicked. The ways and the leading of God are wonderful and admirable, even though our poor eyes may sometimes not be able to see the good things which be sure He yet always does for Israel. Remain faithful to the law, deny thyself even many things that are permitted, be so far as thou canst ever of cheerful and ever joyous temper; and forget not that it is to God, God Eternal, God the Only One, to whom thy soul returns in death.

From the Book of " Pious Souls."
Begun by R. Jehuda b. Samuel of Regensburg.

Be a man's piety ever so great, he can make no claim to recompense at God's hands, were his life to last even for thousands of years; there is none, no, not the least of the benefits conferred on him by God which he could repay. Therefore let no one serve his Creator merely because he hopes for Paradise, but out of pure love for Him and His commandment. Let man in his solitary hours feel the same repugnant shame of evil to the sight of God, as he would to commit it in the sight of men, and let him lay down life freely for Him; for if we do not so, we are of less account in the scale than hireling soldiers who go into battle at the words of command. That our soul may become perfected in righteousness, needs must that we bear griefs and agonies; and never should it cross our minds for an instant to shrink from boldly declaiming that we are Jews.

Mislead no one through thy actions designedly, be he Jew or not-Jew; be not disputatious and quarrelsome with people, whatever be their faith. Be honorable in thy business dealings; do not say that such or such a price has been offered thee for thy wares when the thing is not true, and not behave as though thou hadst a desire to sell what thou hast, when there is no serious thought of doing so in thy mind: such things are unworthy of an Israelite. If one, be he Jew or not-Jew, comes to borrow money from thee, and thou wilt not because of doubt of repayment, say not that thou hast no money.

If a contract be made between Jews and not-Jews, binding to mutual observance and performance, the first must fulfill it even if the last fail to perform that to which they are bound. If a Jew attempt to kill a not-Jew, and the latter only wishes to defend himself, but not in return to kill, we are bound to help him in his self-defense. Injustice must be done to none, whether he belong to our religion or to another. On the worldly possessions of those who oppress the workman, who buy stolen goods, and keep articles decorated with heathen symbols or figures in their household furniture, rests no blessing. They or their children will surely lose all they have. In thy intercourse with not-Jews, be careful to be as wholly sincere as in that with Jews: needst not that thou obtrude on him who is no Jew, argument as to his religious errors, and thou wouldst do better to live on charity, than to abscond with money not thine, to the disgrace of the Jewish faith and name. If one not-Jew seek council of thee, tell him where he will find a true man and not one deceiver in the place whither he repaireth. If thou seest a strange man of another faith about to commit sin, prevent its coming to pass if it be in thy power, and herein let the prophet Jonah be thy model. If an assassin take refuge with thee, give him no protection, even though he be a Jew; if one who bears a heavy burden on his shoulders meet thee on a narrow and difficult path, make way for him, even though he be no Jew. If one not a Jew observe the precepts of the natural (Noachian) moral law, restore to him whatsoever he may have lost, hold him in higher honor than the Israelite who neglects the truth given him by God. For the rest, in most places Jews are not unlike Christians in their morals and usages.

If any one offer thee an amulet, alleging it to be useful in helping to favor or wealth, carry it not, but place thy undivided confidence in God alone. If, when thy plans fail, thou wouldst seek any other Lord than the Eternal thy God, it would be apostasy. If thou canst possibly support thyself with the little thou hast, take not aught from another in order that thou mayest be rich; for few of those who take from others have any happiness in life. No blessing rests on the money of people who clip coin, make a practice of usury, use false weights and measures, and are in general not honest in business; their children and their friends' friends lose their homes at last and have to beg their bread. But many a one falls into poverty because he has looked down upon poor people or has repulsed them with harsh words. If one is able to work, I give him nothing, nothing. It is better to spend on poor people than to lavish in keeping useless foolish things, as birds or other such trifles.

To him who is merciful and good to men, God is merciful and good: the pitiless man is like the cattle of the field which

are indifferent to the sufferings of their kind. There are three
sorts of people for whom we ought to feel especial pain and
sympathy: a reasonable, prudent creature subjected to a crazy
fool; a good man who has to take orders from a bad; and a
noble being dependent upon one of vulgar nature. There are
three to whom we should sternly close our hearts: a cruel
person who does pitiless wrong and vile things, the fool who
rushes on ruin in spite of warning, and the ingrate. Ingratitude is the blackest of faults; it is not to be endured even
towards the dumb creatures whom we use. Worthy of punishment is he, too, who heaps excessive burdens on the carrying
beast, beats and tortures it, twitches a cat by its ears to hurt
it, or plunges his spurs too deep into a horse's flank. A sick
or breeding beast ought to be tenderly dealt with; if a not
dangerous dog runs into thy house, hunt him out with a small
whip that hurts not, but see that thou strike him not with a
heavy stick or pour boiling water over him, or jam him in the
doors, or madden him by any ill-usage. Even worse hath he
to answer for, who deals harshly with serving man or woman.
If the people are good, yet thou needest money, part with
them not to any cruel person who will chastise them with
inhuman severity.

Hear not calumny willingly; seek rather to admonish and
restrain him who complains bitterly to thee of the doings of
another. When thou speakest concerning one, tell the good
thou knowest of him; but do not so in presence of his enemies,
for they would make it opportunity to vent themselves concerning his faults. Praise not one rich man in presence of
another rich man; one author in presence of another author,
and as a rule, never one man of any business in presence of

another whose business is the same; only thou mayest freely give all glory to a God-fearing man in presence of another who fears his God. Make not reply in high-pitched self-asserting tones, but with moderate and sweet, and when thou findest thyself among people who have nothing better to do than to jeer and gibe, leave them as soon and as quickly as thou canst; for mockery leads to want of respect for one's self and others, and that is the high road to an unchaste life. Insist not upon having explanations by word of mouth with one who, as you ought to know, will turn a deaf ear to thy side of the question, or who is likely to become embittered and vengeful owing to such talk.

If a rich man and a poor man be sick, and thou seest all the world going to see the rich man, go thou to the poor one, even though he be ignorant and unlettered. But when thou hast to choose between supplying the needs of a learned man, or counseling the susceptibilities of a poor man, the first case is of the greater urgency; and if it should be that the scholar is also devout and God-fearing, but the poor man not so, then disregard the poor man's feelings altogether, if need be, to mark thy respect for learned piety. Be intimate and work with rather an uneducated man of generous soul than a learned one close-fisted. If thou art in debt, pay thy debts before thou givest alms. If thou requirest one to join with thee in fellowship of study, and knowest of a worthy, reserved and modest disciple of the schools of whom others in reckless high spirits are wont to make mockery, choose and take him to thee, that one who is undeservedly set down may be lifted up to his right place. Make no sign of visible disgust when thou meetest people afflicted with loathsome visible disease; for they are

God's creatures, remember, and healthy as well as sick are all alike dependent upon Him.

Say not, " I will avenge that wrong." Place thy trust in God; He will keep thee. If any one hath deceived thee by false weights, stolen from thee, borne false witness against thee, be not so misguided as to avenge thyself by doing the like. When insult is poured on thee, be thou unmoved, and never permit thy pupils, or those of thy household, to assail with injurious words or blows, when they meet him, one who is doing injury to thee. Expel all envy, all hatred from thy breast; if a fund be making up, and thy name be put down for more than thy possessions warrant, so that richer men pay less than they strictly should, breed not quarrel and mortification for thyself and others by remonstrance and reproach; hold thy peace and busy thyself more than ever with the study of divine things. When thy wife makes thy life heavy for thee, and hatred for her threatens to take possession of thee, then implore the Lord not to give thee another wife, but to turn that one's heart once more back to thee in love.

Let no one be troubled in mind or take up wrong ideas because of the prosperity of wicked people or of such as hold parents in little honor; their end is bad. The reason why good men have an ill lot in life is, lest men should fancy that the good man can only then be good when the world goes well with him. If a congregation has bad men at its head, that is a punishment for not valuing as they should the good men among them. The children of noble, righteous converts to the faith are to be preferred for the marriage tie to children of Jews of nature or conduct not so high.

The ancients of our nation composed works and sent them

forth without their names; they disclaimed to seek recompensing delight for their labor in this lower earthly life. And if there be any one who of pure vanity is minded to perpetuate the memory of himself in some work, very surely he will miss his aim. There was once a rich man, who would build a beautiful synagogue at his own charge alone, and suffered not the congregation to contribute to the pious work, because he would that the memorial should be of him and his posterity alone. But ere he died his children all were dead.

If a father knows his married daughter to be busy and occupied with her husband's affairs, let him not suggest or order her to attend to his own, unless the husband allow of it, postponing his own interests for a while. If a mother hath enjoined some action on her son, and the father come suddenly and say : " Who gave orders that this thing should be done?" let not the son say that it was the mother. For if it should hap that the father in rage should vent an angry curse against his wife, the fault would be laid at the door of the son rather than his own. If a son see an opportunity for some transaction of profit, let him rather miss the chance than rouse his sleeping father, unless he is well assured that the father would be more vexed because the gain was sacrificed than because his sleep was broken. He who spends substance in supporting other than parents and relations will reap nothing but ingratitude, while his property will fall to those of his own blood at last. If a father treats one son well, another ill, it is the latter who is very likely to succeed to his possessions. Let one who hath never known parents, but only elder brothers, render the respect and honor due to father and mother unto these.

Parents may not hinder a son's marriage that he may continue to work for them; let him take a wife and remain with them still. If he can find no wife at the place where his parents live, and these be aged and need his care, let him not leave that city: and if, taking a wife, he can no longer care for such helpless father and mother, let him remain unwedded. If he can pay for the support and care of his parents, then he hath a right to seek wife and settle elsewhere, only let him see to it that they are not such as are repugnant to the parents' feelings. If his choice hath fallen on a worthy girl of honorable parentage, but his father or mother wish to force him to take one not worthy, because her relatives offer money, he needs herein by no means to yield to his parents' wishes, for their proceeding is blameworthy. Parents must by no means, on no account whatever, strike a grown-up son, curse him, or so move him to wrath that he forget himself and with whom he is dealing. If children are hopelessly divided in feeling, a father does well if he arrange all things concerning his possessions while he lives, and place property and children alike, if they be minors, with all legal form under guardianship and trust.

Let not a quite young man take to wife one who hath reached forty years; let no girl be married against her will to an elderly man or one whom she cannot love. It is a thing highly to be disapproved that elderly men should dye gray hairs black to deceive young girls as to their years. In most cases bad parents beget bad children. If parents have no scruples about false coin and false weights, the sons are apt to commit the same crimes. If we see about us so many uneducated and ignorant, but descendants of people of high instruction, this is the fault of parents whom worldly interest hath led to form connections with unlearned persons. There was a man who lived a poor and hard life, to whom a wealthy woman was offered in marriage ; he refused her, for her brothers were unworthy and he dreaded lest his children by her might be the same. So far as legal duty goes, a man indeed need not abstain from wedding a wife so connected, just as he may repudiate his wife for reasons that seem trifling and inadequate ; but many things are permitted by the law, the doing of which may lay upon a man the rendering of a heavy account some day or other.

On the day of the last judgment those who are of kindred virtue and merit will find themselves in final companionship with each other. The father then ceases to mourn and grieve over the son that had left him ; for the joys of Paradise and the rapturous delight felt in meeting the radiance of God's countenance will send into oblivion all the anguish of the earthly life.

R. MOSES OF EVREUX (1240).

Above all let a man be on his guard against wrath : for the powers of hell do what they will with the blindly angry man. To guard against angry feeling is the way to reach humility, and in doing so thou wilt find it needful to be watchful lest thou rise into self-exaltation, and one who is self-exalted offends against God, with whose Being only is the thought of exaltation compatible. Be, therefore, gentle and humble in thy ways and demeanor, speak freely and accessibly with every one ; go about with head not held too high, let thine eyes look somewhat away from people, but let thine heart look them straight in the face. In discourse with folk look not with intrusive, fixed eyes into theirs; consider and treat every one, rich or poor, as one greater than thyself, to whom respectful conduct is due. If thou knowest that thou art wealthier, more powerful, or more educated than he, none the less must thou treat him with all honorable respect, remembering that he may be a better man than thou at his heart, and in case when thou wouldst offend wittingly and voluntarily he might only do so in spite of himself. In all thy doings, in all thy resolves, forget not that thou standest in the presence of God, of Him whose glory fills the whole earth, of whose majesty thou art the subject and creature. Speak, therefore, when thou dost speak, with voice somewhat hushed; fear Him as the servant fears his lord. Let there be no man before whose face thou wouldst not scruple to do wrong things; be lowly before every man; answer every man's call with not too raised a voice, but quietly as one always in presence of the schoolmaster who teacheth him how to live. Busy thyself as oft and as much as possible with the study of divine things, not to know them only, but to do; and when thou closest the book look round thee, look within thee to see if thine hand can find aught to execute answering to something thou hast learned. Whenever night falls, whenever day dawns, search well into thy dealings, of what sort they be; so will thy whole life be one long atoning expiating day. When thou prayest, keep all thought other than prayer far from thy soul; reflect upon the words of thy prayer ere they pass thy lips, so that thou bringest a mind prepared and in good order for speaking with thy God. Yea, do this even on all other occasions, and even in the taking of thy meat and drink be not over hasty and quick, for even that partakes of the nature of a fault. Go not about with people who indulge without restraint in mocking views of things. So shall all thy dealings be righteous, and thy prayer such as God can hear and answer.

R. Moses b. Jacob of Coucy (1245).

From Semag.

Those who lie freely even to not-Jews and steal from them, belong to the class of blasphemers; for it is due to their guilt that some say, the Jews have no binding law. If things go well with Israelites, they should not lose their heads and forget God, and ascribe all successes to their own industry and skill. Let no one, indeed, exalt himself because of any advantage he hath, be it money, or beauty, or cleverness; let him be and remain before man humble, before God thankful. The divine mind dwells with the man of humble spirit, and he who keepeth himself lowly doth as well as though he offered up all the burnt-sacrifice that ever was enjoined. The wishes of the humble man are fulfilled even before he uttereth any words of request. But, on the contrary, people of haughty overbearing temper do but inspire aversion; surely they will have no part or lot in Zion's future joy.

Either in commerce or in any other of life's business, dare not to deceive any man, of whatsoever religion he be, by word or deed; rather, indeed, point out to the buyer wherein thy goods are wanting.

It is because man is half angel, half brute, that his inner life witnesses such bitter war between such unlike natures. The brute in him clamors for sensual joy and things in which there is only vanity; but the angel resists and strives to make him know that meat, drink, sleep, are but means whereby the body may be made sufficient for the study of the truths, and the doing of the will of God. Not until the very hour of death can it be certain or known which of the two hath won the victory.

The highest service that can be rendered God is to love Him, purely because our Creator. Circumcision, Sabbath, Tefillin, are the three symbolic marks of the Israelite which testify that he is a servant of God. And he who is but a novice in the fear of God will do well to say audibly each day, as he rises: "This day will I be a faithful servant of the Almighty; be on my guard against wrath, falsehood, hatred, quarrelsomeness; will look not too closely at women, and forgive those who wound me. For whoso forgives is forgiven in his turn; hard-heartedness and a temper that will not make up quarrels are a heavy burden of sin, unworthy of an Israelite.

BERACHJA HA-NAKDAN (ABOUT 1260).

From The Book of Fables.

Prefer the possession of one thing to the mere expectation of two; a small certainty is better than a large peradventure. Be a servant among noble-minded men, rather than a chieftain over the vulgar. The good repute of the first will reflect itself on thee; but the contempt felt for those over whom thou hast direction, will soon extend itself equally to thee. If thou too earnestly seek pre-eminence and power, be sure that will flee thee; but if thou bearest thyself in this world like a guest receiving its hospitality, men will try to find for thee a place of honor and a place of profit.

It is an evil trait of very many men that they treat with little deference those who in truth deserve more honor than themselves : too often they bear a grudge against a known good man and never come near him save when they want some service from him. The man of merit hath too often to bend his back before men of vulgar soul, and because he only knows how to wield a good blade, while they are in command.

The proud cedar is felled, while the humble shrub is left alone ; fire ascends and goes out, water descends and is not lost. Exalt not thyself because of beauty and wealth over neighbor and brother ; for, so doing, thou givest provender to loathsome hate, and the poor man, whom thou hast looked down on, may bear away the palm of victory easily from thee.

He who would preserve his dignity, will perish rather than surrender his honor : prefers freedom and content to all luxury at the prison of a stranger's table.

Give thy love equally to all thy children ; often does the hope placed on those preferred turn out mere illusion, while all thy happiness and joy come from the one whom thou hast disregarded or neglected.

From the Tosafot of the Pentateuch.

(Second Half of the 13th Century.)

What a man spends on the poor when he is in full health is gold ; when sick, silver ; what he provides for them in his last will, copper.

If thou return not his pledged goods to the poor man at eventide, thou deservest not that thy pledge, thy soul placed each night in the hands of God, should be returned to thee at daylight.

Unmeasured drinking of wine brings poverty, shame, quarrels; leads to calumnious talk, inchastity, murder, to the loss of freedom, of honor, of understanding.

Power and wealth acquired without true personal merit, or without the fear of God, take wings and fly. Both these things, as well as mental cleverness, are gifts of God, therefore let no man glory because he possesses them. The only thing we, as free agents, really possess in full inalienable right, is upright walking in the fear of God; and it is because that is so, that we can glory in the knowledge of God.

ANONYMOUS (ABOUT 1300)
(*From Kol Bo, No.* 67.)

When a new spirit of atoning repentance really comes over a man, so that he would fain be pure from sin as a new-born babe, let him read every day some prayer that calls to mind such resolve and wish. As soon as he riseth in the morning, let him review all his dealings with others, and be anxiously careful not to do any wrong thing before he sits down to his day's first food. But, should it so hap that something of the kind hath befallen, let him confess his error, without delay, in prayer, and he will be protected against a repetition of his fault; for he will be ashamed to stand as a liar before God, and that will be his guard. If he hath persevered in his good resolves, let him thank his Creator for it, who hath stood by him, and helped him to be pure a while. Let him do the same before the evening meal, and before his nightly sleep, and continue it daily, month by month, till a year hath gone by, so that he may be strong in good resolve, and freed from his evil habits. But let him never cease to mourn over his earlier sins, and let him impose upon himself many works of atonement and repentance, and, if he be too weak for this, let him strengthen himself thereto by moderation and renunciation. Habitually to renounce delicacies at the table is a better barrier than fasting against excess in matter of food. Let him bow his spirit to divine truth, his body to the law; let him fulfill the commandments earnestly and actively, even when false shame might, perhaps, induce him to neglect them. Then let him not blindly fear that the atonement he is making cannot possibly outweigh his sins; for when one repents truly and with true grief, the evil that he hath done is no more thought of, and the repentant sinner even excels the sinless just. Well is it for him who, even out of all men's sight, fulfills the will of God; who without murmuring suffers pain and trouble for his faith; the day will come when he shall be freed from his griefs.

R. Ascher b. Iechiel of Germany (Died 1327).

(*From his Testament.*)

Be not ready to quarrel; avoid oaths and passionate adjurations, excess of laughter and outbursts of wrath; they disturb and confound the reason of a man. Avoid all dealings wherein there is a lie; utter not the name of God superfluously to no useful end, or in places dirty or defiled. Cut from under thee all mere human supports, make not gold the foremost longing of thy life; for that is the first step to idol worship, a heathen religion. Nay, rather wander in all humility before thy Creator, and where thou seest His will to be so, give up thy money at once; He can more than replace it. Rather give money than words; and as to ill words, see that thou place them in the scale of understanding before they leave thy lips. What hath been uttered in thy presence, even though not told as secret, let it not pass from thee to others. And if one tell thee a tale, say not to him that thou hast heard it all before.

Sleep not late with the indolent man; rise with the sun and the singing bird. Be not a glutton or a hard drinker; it might lead thee to forget thy Maker. Do not fix thy eyes too much on one who is far above thee in wealth, but on those who are behind thee in worldly fortune. Only in respect of the service and the fear of God look up to the great, and never on the insignificant. Take pleasure in being warned from wrong and set to right, seek for good counsel and for instruction cheerfully; exalt not thyself proudly above men; do it not; rather remain the dust for all to tread on. Speak not to others in hard and supercilious manner; be not obstinate and self-willed, but abide in the fear of God.

Lift not up thine hand against thy neighbor, yea, though he insult thy parents before thee; speak no ill of anybody, mock and vilify no human being. If any one speak what is unbecoming, give him no rude answer. Let no one ever hear thy speech because it is so loud on the street; cry not out like a brute beast, but speak decorously. Put no one to open-shame; misuse not thy power against any one; who can tell whether thou wilt not some day be powerless thyself? Hunt not for honors, and place not thyself in any place that belongs to thee not. Never cease to acquire friends; avoid making even one enemy. When a companion is of approved truth, spare no pains in attaching him to thee and cherish him carefully; but flatter him not and say no untrue word to him.

Do not struggle vaingloriously for the small triumph of showing thyself in the right, and a wise man in the wrong:

thou art not one whit the wiser therefor.   Be not angry or
unkind to any one for trifles, lest thou make thyself enemies
unnecessarily.   Strive not to screw out the secrets of others;
do not refuse things of mere obstinacy to thy fellow-citizens,
rather put thy will below their wishes.   Avoid, as much as may
be, bad men, men of persistent angry feeling, fools; thou canst
get nothing from their company but shame.   Never address
thy remarks to an utterly irrational man of whom thou knowest
that he cannot take them in.   Be and remain grateful to any
one who hath helped thee to thy bread; be sincere and true
with every one, even those who are not Jews; be the first to
extend courteous greeting to every one, whatever be his faith;
provoke not to wrath one of another belief than thine.

Receive kindly travellers who seek thy house; supply their
needs when there; lead them on their way with kind, good
words.   Make not a practice of sleeping elsewhere than under
thine own roof; be on thy guard against drunkenness, and
then thou wilt not have to repent vulgar conduct and unfitting
speech.   Never be violently angry with thy wife, and if haply
thy left hand had repulsed her, let thy right draw her quickly
to thy heart again.   Make not light of her in thy dealings with
her, but hold her in all respect and honor; so shalt thou keep
her from the thought and deed of sin.   See that thou force
not those of thy household to over-fear of thee.   Much misery
and wrong hath sprung ere now therefrom.

When thou takest food or drink, give God thanks before and
after enjoying it; when thou utterest the name of God, cover
thy head.   Before prayer, before meals, wash thee thy hands;
let thy demeanor be reverent, not in the synagogue alone, but
in thy home; even with thy wife thou dost not well to speak

with levity of unedifying things. Before thou eatest, before thou goest to thy bed, occupy thyself for some set time with the law, and let thy discourse at table be on matter which it contains. Prayer is the soul's service to God; see that thou be reverent in prayer above all; but speak audibly the words that thou mayest hear thy prayer and know that thou art praying.

R. Eliazar b. Samuel Ha-Levi (Died 1327 in Mayence).
From his Testament.

I lay on my children my injunction or advice that at morning, immediately after prayer, they read some passages in the Pentateuch or Psalms, or do some work of mercy. In their intercourse with others, Jews or not-Jews, let them be conscientious and anxious to do right, amiable and accommodating, and never speak when speech is superfluous; so will they be guarded against uttering words of calumny or mockery against others.

From the Book of Morals (15th Century).

The thread on which the different good qualities of human beings are strung, as pearls, is—the fear of God. When the fastenings of this fear are unloosed, the pearls roll in all directions and are lost one by one. But without taking a high degree in morality we can neither enter into possession of the learning of divine things nor fulfill positive precepts; nay, even a single grave moral fault may be the ruin of all other advantages, as when, for example, one is always seeking to set off his own excellence by bringing into prominence his neighbor's failings. It is just as with wine, the best of which may escape from a

vessel through one little hole overlooked. But there are but
few men who recognize this to be true in their own case;
they see the lofty ladder they have to mount; they cannot see
that their feet suffice not for the ascent. Or they have no
notion what a treasure they possess in their own souls, and
recklessly sell their house and all the treasures it contains.
But the heart is like a tablet as yet unwritten; fools scratch
it all over and ruin it; only the wise know how to fill it with '
suitable matter.

A habit to be most especially inculcated and commended,
is that of cleanliness. Clothing, bed, table, table-furniture,
especially those used for food, indeed all and everything that
we ever take in our hands, let it all be clean, sweet, pure; the
body above and beyond all, made in the image of God, that
ought never to be defiled by dirt.

It is wretched pride when one is always thinking others as
lower than himself, and that his own opinion is always better than
others'. All progress is thereby made wholly impossible; such
a one does things only for approval of men, not because God
wills he should; is always seeking thanks for what he does,
takes delight in others' crouching as inferiors before him. A
person of that kind is like a very superior article of food burnt
by the cook, and which therefore has to be sent away from
table. The sweeter self-love makes our own ignorance to us,
the more bitter do we become towards others, the less acces-
sible to all opportunity of reform.

Be reasonable and modest in thy dealings and intercourse
with men; speak reasonably and modestly with every one,
and treat him fairly well. Practice humility, even toward in-
mates of thine house, poor people, subordinates. Be not chary

but kind of speech with widows and converts; put up willingly
with discomfort from their talk; reply not when men scold
thee; be deferential to men of learning or piety; thoughtful
and circumspect towards thy scholars and disciples, and never
be tired of repeating things over and over again to them, that
they may understand them aright. Never be ashamed to
learn, even from less men than thyself. He who is humble
toward everybody, pleases and wins confidence, and every one
wishes to be even as he is. But the more of worldly or other
good things thou hast, the greater let thy humility be, all the
more do thou pay respect to men, and abound in kindness
towards them.

Let a man be never ashamed to execute the commands of .
religion, even though he be mocked therefor; never ashamed
to confess the truth, to set another man right, to put a question
to a teacher when something is not well understood. But let
a man be well on his guard against putting others to shame, or
lay bare wantonly the failings of a neighbor, or give him a dis-
honorable nickname, or address him by such. Never tell any
one that such a one wished to give his daughter to thee in
marriage, and thou wouldst not have her. Never put in words
anything which can call up a blush on thine own cheek, or make
another's grow pale.

It is very vexatious, very wrong, to keep up and support
evil men; but to keep down good men, and thrust them from
thee, it is frightful weakness to do so. But genuine compas-
sion and pity highly become and adorn the Israelite; be pitiful,
therefore, even to thy cattle, and give them food even before
thou thyself eatest; and be careful that on no account thou
give even brute beast unnecessary pain. The words of Scrip-

ture, " the tender mercy of the wicked is cruel," refer to such as exact heavy returns from poor men for favors received.

Be tender-hearted towards bondsmen who are not Jews. Make not their labor too heavy for them; treat them not as though they were of no account whatever, by words of contempt or blows; even in dispute with a serving man speak affably, and listen to what he hath to say. Our ancient teachers relieved the slave from all responsibility to criminal law, and provided anxiously for his needs, even as for their own.

When thou seest that men are not what they should be, do not rejoice over the fact, but grieve, for thou shouldst pray even on thine enemy's behalf that he serve his God.

On thy business and affairs let not thy trust and dependence be placed, but on God alone. He it is who supports thee, and those affairs are nothing more than the means He applies to thy support. It is not the iron, but the force that moves the iron, that fells the tree. Think not, then, when thou art supporting thyself by some earnings of thy calling, that without these earnings thou must needs starve; but put thy entire confidence in God, who will support thee in some other manner; for He hath many messengers always ready for his service. He helps in small ways, and also in great. Therefore put not thy confidence wholly in any human creature, on whom thou art dependent for thy bread, but think and say boldly that God alone it is who holds thee up, He alone it is whose eyes lead us, poor blind creatures, in our path, we who all stand in such need the one of the other. So will even he who supports thee be not overproud to thee for doing so; for he, too, is a blind man among the blind.

Forget never the merits that thou lackest, but forget always

the good that thou hast done ; set down thy failings, thy faults
in thy book, but not the benefits thou hast conferred. Forget
the wounds inflicted on thee by others, and when thou prayest,
forget thou earthly things.

Thirty things there are thou shouldst bring to mind each
twice a day, and take them seriously to heart: (1.) God made
thee out of nothing, a being set over all created things, and
that from pure love to thee, for he owed thee no obligation to
do it. (2.) It is to God's goodness thou art indebted for
sound limbs and entire. How deeply wouldst thou feel thyself indebted to a physician who should heal a single limb,
but it is God who keeps thee all thy limbs intact. (3.) He
gave thee understanding. (4.) Holy Writ and doctrine.
(5.) The means whereby they are understood. (6.) All
creatures follow the will of their Creator; beast and plant, sun
and earth, do what they ought to do, and man should be
ashamed to let his members bo used to overstep the laws. (7.)
If a mere serving-man fears and loves the master that does him
good, how much more should man recognize the sovereignty of
God, and be of humble bearing towards Him. (8.) Faithful
servants spend energy and attention to execute as best they
can their master's commands, and are careful to choose their
words when they approach him with words of gratitude or
other. So let thy service to God, both without and within, be
reverential and anxious. (9.) Fulfill the commandments out
of pure love, neither on account of men nor for reward. (10.)
Think well over thy bearing towards thy Creator, whether
there be nothing wherein thou hast to better, to perfect thyself. (11.) Thou art indefatigable to obtain money, that possession uncertain at best; what labor, what anxiety is being

spent unspairingly; is there any for the welfare of thy immortal soul? (12.) Thou puttest thyself in fine garments to please men; forget not that God looks in thy heart: adorn that well in honor of Him. (13.) If thou art clever and rich, do good according to the measure of thy powers, and be not idle in that regard under the pretext that thou waitest until.thou art still more clever and wealthy. (14.) God has given us assurance of his love for all time, and will not thrust us from Him, even in the enemy's country (Levit. xxvi. 44), therefore return of love is but His simple due. (15.) For the distant journey to which thou mayest at all times suddenly be called make timely provision. (16.) Keep thy soul always pure; thou knowest not the moment when it may be required of thee. Many a young, many a strong man hath gone before thee to his home. (17.) Seek solitude, it preserves from many a sin, or otherwise keep to the society of the pious only. (18.) Be grateful for, not blind to the many, many sufferings which thou art spared; thou art no better than those who have been searched out and racked by them. (19.) Thy possession is not thy property, but a deposit with thee only; and if it be God's will, soon falls to another man. Therefore look down on no poor man, for the more that thou hast is no merit of thine own. (20.) Thou art a being of earth, and yet hast knowledge in some measure of God, and dominion over the other creatures; thank, therefore, and pay homage to the Giver. (21.) Accustom thyself to do good, that it may become an easy thing to thee, and implore therein the divine assistance. (22.) Be lovable in word and deed towards men. (23.) Be not blind, but open-eyed to the great wonders of nature, familiar objects though they be to thee, of every day. But men are more wont to be astonished at the sun's eclipse than at his unfailing rise. (24.) Be not content with the studies of thy youthful years, but think of and study truth and what thy action should be in the years of thy maturity, and thine insight will gain in strength and depth. (25.) Let thy yearning for the delights of the life to come be stronger than thy clinging to the life of earth. (26.) Let thy soul fear the chastisement of the King of Kings. (27.) Accept grief and pain with resignation and love; be they never so keen, they are yet milder than the punishment which is thy due. (28.) Be ready to give back thyself, wife, children, all possession, to the Lord that gave them thee, and be ever willing to bear that which He lays upon thee. (29.) It is often the case that one human being is worth a hundred others. Never because of his body, but because of his spirit, his mental insight, his moral worth. So build ever higher and higher the edifice of thy soul, for all merit takes its origin there only. A man, strong, healthy, beautiful, but all astray in mind, is worth nothing, while an ill-favored man, weak in body, but abounding in mental gifts, may rise to highest honors. (30.) When any one comes into a strange land, where he knows, and is known of, none, and its ruler takes him up, supports him, makes him one of his servants, sees that he is well rewarded for his service, and does not suffer him to forget, in the time of his well-being, that, some day, the date of which is not yet fixed, he will have to quit the country again, surely such a one would be deferential and faithful in the service of such a master, and specially love those who are strangers there like himself, and do all possible good for that country, where no one save its king was so good and kind to him. Well, just so did man come as a stranger into this world, and no one is his supporter save God, and no one there is so pitiful and tender to him as He who made him.

Put no one to open shame; injure no one's feelings who has any bodily failing, or on whose family rests a stain. If thou sittest next to such a one, speak not of such deficiency or fault, even in reference to other than himself. If any one relate thee something known already, be silent till he has finished; for, granting that he tells thee nothing new, he had the pleasure of believing that he did. Touch not the subject of a quarrel that is ended, thou mayest fire the dying embers afresh.

Luxury and good living, idleness and sitting at wine, lead to unrestraint of soul, and so to evil speaking and mockeries. People of this kind sit there and make merry over poor men and pious; but their mockeries strike at God, and at the works of God. Or else they think themselves the only clever ones of earth, and make a mock of other people's proceedings, because they are not their own, and never listen to any advice of better things.

He who flatters a bad man falls into his or his descendants' hands; flatter not either relative or child when they are not following after good things. Especially ought a chief man of any community, a judge, an administrator of charitable funds to be a true and not false man, for personal interest or any other reason smooth and insincere of tongue. But worthiest of blame is that flattery whose aim is to seduce a human being into wrong. Desire for worldly honors, self-interest, vanity, these are the things which make men hypocrites and false. How many a teacher and scholar in our day are taken in this snare. To make their power sure, to turn the lives of people to their own account, they not only refrain from rebuking where they should, but play false, or put on false appearances, by keeping silence when they ought to speak in honor of the truth.

Five offenses are hard ever to repair; a curse launched at a multitude of men ; sharing the spoil of thieves ; keeping as your own, lost things; oppression of the poor ; rendering corrupt judgment. Five sins are not thought much of, but yet are grave : to abuse the hospitality of poor people ; to turn to one's own use the deposit of a poor man ; to look on beautiful women whose society is forbidden; to rejoice at another's disgrace ; to suspect the innocent. Five bad habits are hard to get rid of : chattering, calumny, angry temper, suspicion, associating with bad people.

The aim of all thought, the highest of all merits, is love to God ; let this thrust into the background all other love. All our dealings with the delights of life, whether of enjoyment or renunciation, should lead the soul to turn freely and fully to its Creator, so that it may participate in the light on high, overcoming the desires of the body. Love of that sort is bound up with a joy that causes all the pleasant things of this world to fade into nothingness ; in comparison with the raptures of that love all other delights pale, even those we have in our children. To love God so that His service, and that only, fills our hearts, so that if need come, we sacrifice ourselves freely and unhesitatingly for it, that is the sort of fear of God which Holy Writ sets before our eyes. Well is it with the soul, blessings on the soul that reaches the enchantments of this joy. The divine spirit rests only on those filled with such joy, only when they were thus sublimely glad had the prophets the gift of the spirit; the soul made holy by such yearning for the source from which it sprang is destined to enter into the appointed place where life glows and shines with a fire that shall never be quenched.

JEWISH MARRIAGE

IN POST-BIBLICAL TIMES.

A Study in Archæology.

By Dr. JOSEPH PERLES.

Jewish Marriage

IN POST-BIBLICAL TIMES.

A STUDY IN ARCHÆOLOGY.

By Dr. JOSEPH PERLES.

—— .

HE legal and other consequences worked by marriage on persons or property, the modes of performing the marriage ceremony, and everything indeed connected with it, will always be found to be closely correlated to the conception formed of marriage among a people, and to be best explained thereby. Where marriage is regarded as a holy institution, as the keystone of genuine morality, as the delightful union of two kindred souls, yielding themselves to each other freely in love and duty, on a ground where they are spiritually and morally equal, there too we shall find usages religious and social, connected with the solemn celebration of the marriage ceremony; there we shall find a sense of sanctity and consecration in its performance, and a joyousness among all concerned, not boisterous, but measured and touching deeply the inner life. The position assigned to woman by the general feeling and opinion is here the determining element and stamps itself unmistakably on all that is done ; we may certainly know by inspection of the marriage ceremonial whether the wife enters wedlock as dumb creatures involuntarily submit to the yoke, or whether she holds out her hand as an independent person acting of free will, to a husband of her choice.

Applying this to the solemnities connected with marriage among the Jewish people, and estimating them in comparison with those practiced among others, we have at the outset to bear steadily in mind the very different character borne by marriage among Hebrews and other nations. That in Jewish marriage morality at its highest and human, but above all, feminine, dignity were consulted, expressed, and realized in every word and gesture is a fact that has been so proved by repeated exposition that we need not here enlarge upon the subject. For quite lately a hand entirely competent to the task has amply shown that " among the Jewish people marriage was rooted in morality, and grew to the height at which it became so noble and ennobling entirely by sustenance it drew from moral ideas." (Frankel, " Outline of Mosaico-Talmudic Marriage Law," p. xi.) To quote one only of the countless utterances of the Rabbis upon the exalted significance of marriage, let us hear the opinion of one of these sages. " How sublime the dignity of marriage is we may know, for in the Pentateuch, in the Prophets, in the Hagiographers it is announced to be of divine institution ; in one passage, Laban and Bethuel answered—This thing proceeds from none lower than God (Gen. xxiv. 50); concerning Samson we read, his father and mother knew not that the thing had been brought about by God (Judges xiv. 4); and in Proverbs, in fine, it is written,

House and land are inheritance from ancestors, but a thoughtful wife is God's own gift." Marriage, indeed, was so serious, so sacred in the eyes of the Rabbis that they declared the bridegroom purged of sin by reason of his entering that holy state, thus giving to the ceremony the full effect of the prayer and fasting of the great Atoning Day. Monogamy, the only marriage which develops genuine and deep morality, which, even as early as in the narrative of creation, is pronounced the real marriage of human nature, and which in biblical Jewish times only temporarily made way for polygamy, that accident of climate, monogamy was the almost universal Jewish rule in post-biblical times; and R. Gerschom, surnamed Light of the Exile, met with but little opposition worth the name when he issued his famous condemnatory decree against plural marriage. While among Greeks woman was known as the " progenitrix," γυνή (from γείνα), among Romans as the " prolific," *femina* (related to *fecundus*), in the Jewish world she was known as " Ish-shah," equivalent, in moral as well as literal etymology, to the Ish : man ; and it is she to whom the Scriptures principally refer in speaking of a *man's house*, בֵּיתוֹ זוּ אִשְׁתּוֹ . While the classical nations regarded Hera, the goddess of marriage, as ᾱυγία, the patroness that is of the marriage yoke, whose unseen hand placed it on married necks, and marriage as a yoking together of two people, *conjugium*, each one of whom is σύζυξ or ὁμόζυξ, yokefellow ; while the Arabs and Persians give to wedlock a still more hateful designation, the Hebrew, on the other hand, calls betrothal by a name deeply significant of the very soul of marriage, *Kiddushin*, or sanctification, and gives to marriage itself the noble appellation of *Hilloola*, or song of exultant praise.

4

Where the ground thought was so dignified, everything connected with the performance and solemnization of marriage could not but bear the marks of exultation and purity. How abundantly true this is of the *juridical* aspect of the matter, the Talmud testifies abundantly, and is shown by Frankel with the utmost acuteness and learning. In this paper we intend to confine ourselves to showing, in a brief space, how this was so in regard to the solemnities attending the marriage ceremony among Jews in post-biblical times.

Betrothal precedes the marriage, which is brought about by the courtship of the bridegroom, as well as, in a measure, by the mediation of third parties. The Talmud gives an instance of a rejected suit. When R. Eliazar died, another doctor of the law sought his widow in marriage, but was refused with the remarkable speech: " One without the sanctuary may not use a wine-cup that has served a holy man whose place was within." That, occasionally, betrothals took place while the bride and bridegroom were still unknown to each other, is proved by the observation of the Talmud that no one ought to marry a wife without having personal knowledge of her. On certain days of the year, there were numerously attended balls at which young people freely danced with each other, and these afforded Jewish girls an opportunity of being freely sought, and, in due measure, of freely giving themselves in marriage. On the fifteenth day of the month Ab and on the day of Atonement, the young ladies, all clad alike in white, that there might be no distinction between the wealthy and others, went out in groups to the wine gardens, formally invited the young men to dance with them, and half foolishly, half in earnest, demanded their hands in marriage.

And these charming candidates for matrimony stated their different claims as best they could; those distinguished for personal beauty dwelt upon that; those of high birth made all they could of noble blood and its influence upon strict fidelity to the marriage bond, while Nature's step-children, who could plead no merits derived from personal appearance, enlarged upon the transitory character of physical advantages and the enduring value of morality.

Betrothal was celebrated with a family banquet at which sometimes the expenditure was very lavish. The apartments were brilliantly lighted up, couches were placed around the walls, guests went in and out in great numbers; the women sat at the spinning-wheel and sang in joyous chorus, "Such a one and such a one are this day given in betrothal." In the so-called and so frequently mentioned progamcia, a word plainly Greek, we seem to have a festival in honor of the marriage, but celebrated some time before it. The German Jews of the middle ages begin this preliminary festival, which they called " *Spinn-holz*," on the Saturday preceding the wedding day. It is to be gathered from several allusions in the Rabbinical writing that certain days were regarded as especially fortunate for the solemnization of marriage, and that it was even an occasional practice to draw the bridegroom's horoscope to determine the wedding day. The Spanish Jews followed Greek precedent in regarding the full moon as a preferential time for weddings. There is reason also to suppose that it was not infrequent there to place on the bride's neck an amulet, to preserve against the " evil eye."

The *status* of betrothed people was one of exceptional honor and respect, and they enjoyed certain privileges in public wor-

ship and social gatherings. The relation of God to the Jewish
people is again and again typified in the Bible and by the
Rabbis by that of persons betrothed in wedlock. The greeting
given to the Sabbath in prayer and used at its moment of
beginning is similar to that given to a beloved bride.* The
bride had a chair of honor specially assigned to her, and was
carried through the city in full dress upon a handsome
palanquin, which was borne on the shoulders of men of the
highest social position. Sometimes the bride was placed on
horseback or on an elephant, and so taken to the house where
the marriage was to be performed. The Jews of the middle
ages used, following the custom of their land and time, to
meet the happy couple with a handsomely ordered cavalcade,
and hold a brief tournament in their honor; and the Rabbis
lay down that any damage done to person in these encounters
need not be the subject of compensation. It was a duty, par-
taking even of religious obligation, to join in songs of praise
of the bride and bridegroom, to join festive marriage processions, and help to stimulate the gaiety of guests attending the
celebration. King Agrippa once joined the cortége attending
a bride to her marriage with the remark, "My head wears a
crown at all times, and therefore I think it well to pay homage
to one who wears it only for the brief hour." According to
Rabbinical precept, the study of the law might properly be
interrupted to join in the songs of a passing marriage procession. R. Jehuda b. Ilai once even bade his disciples, who, we

---

* Used here, observe. in the German sense of betrothed woman. The Germans have never fallen into the confusion of so calling a person after she is
married: a real confusion of thought and terms, for no limit of time can be
assigned after wedlock when the appellation should properly cease.—*Translator.*

may believe, were nothing loth, to leave the lecture-room and add their numbers to a bridal cortége, and he did it on ethical grounds which he quite seriously set forth to them. R. Jehuda Hanasi, observing that a marriage procession was passing, made his students go and follow the pair, telling them that the practical observance of the law was better than its theoretic study. R. Tryphon, too, once noticed, when in his professional chair, a *pompa nuptialis.* He stopped it and had the bride brought into his house, and made his mother and consort put her into a bath, anoint her and put on her some ornaments, and accompany her with joyous steps in some sort of dance to the house of the groom.

According to the opinion of many students of the text in the 45th Psalm, we have preserved for us a marriage song of the loveliest kind. The Talmud has preserved fragments of others. "Away with all thy purchased aids to beauty, She needs them not, our sweet gazelle-eyed girl!" R. Jehuda bar Ilaï and R. Samuel b. Yizchak, in a sort of religious ecstasy, danced once before a bride, waving myrtle branches and uttering songs in her praise. R. Acha once actually took a bride in his arms and invited her to dance with him. The rigid Shammaites were averse to the practice of pouring out rhetorical praise in honor of a bride; but in the eyes of Hillel's followers poetry was a need of nature, and their system recognized it as a legitimate thing. Where nature is given so free a play, the bridal couple were sometimes, as we might expect, the subject of the people's jests and wit, and the gossips stuck their little sharp points into the whole transaction. The Midrasch to Psalm 24 has this: "Once when the people saw a solemn marriage procession where the groom was handsome, but the bride ill-favored, they said to one another, That young fellow's palanquin is a coffin, they are going to bury him alive." And when they saw it the other way, a charming girl by the side of a misshapen groom, they cried out, There's the Beast going to eat up Beauty." There was a teasing question which persons sometimes put to a young husband about his wife's behavior, very elliptical in form; "Is it 'whoso hath found,' or is it, 'I have found,'" where the allusion was to two verses of Scripture: "Whoso hath found a wife hath found his happiness" (Prov. xviii. 22), and, "I have found that a wife is as bitter as death." Something much more serious which at times occurred was the application of the so-called *Kezazah*, the ceremonial in which the connections of a bridegroom in case of a *mésalliance* gave formal expression of their displeasure, and which is described as of the following kind. When the member of a family married beneath himself or one unworthy, his relatives and family brought a vessel filled with all sorts of fruits to some public place, broke it up, and spoke thus to the bystanders: "Brethren of Israel, our relative N. N. has maried a woman unworthy, and the thought tortures us that his descendants should some day form part of our family; take this act therefore as a sign for all future time that his posterity are shut out from and belong not to ours." Whereupon the children present gathered up the fruits that had fallen from the vessel, and said in chorus, "N. N. has been put out of his family."

At the wedding, the bridal pair appeared in most elaborate costume, attended by bridesmaids and groomsmen (paranymphs), and soon a crowd gathered from all quarters. The head of the happy bride was adorned with garlands of roses, myrtles, olive-branches, and ornamental reeds, with ornaments of gold or crystal, and silk from Miletus. There was many a grave doctor of the law who would allow no other hands than his to weave the garlands for his daughter-bride. That the full stream of delight might be in some degree checked or qualified by more serious thought, it was customary to throw ashes on the bridegroom's head, in sad commemoration of the destruction of Jerusalem; or later, in Spain, to encircle it with a garland of olive twigs. Young maidens went to meet the bridal couple with torches, the *faces nuptiales* of the Romans. As R. Nathan b. Jechiel, of Rome, informs us, it was the usage still of the Arabian Jews in the middle ages to carry in front of the bridal procession a number of staffs which supported a vessel carrying combustible materials, which were fired while the procession was going on. In a proclamation of Peter the Second of Castile (1338), the patrols of the city are instructed not to interfere with Jews when they passed the open place in front of the citadel, the Cassero, with their marriage processions, and the document specifies that it is not necessary to entitle to this immunity that every one present should be carrying a torch, but enough if the first or leading person of the cortége does so.

In honor of the young couple, wine and oil were poured from jars filled with them, on the passage towards the house where the wedding was held, and the folks threw nuts and roasted ears of corn about. It was customary to carry in front of a virgin bride a vessel filled with so-called Theruma wine, as a symbol of her chastity and youthful freshness. In Babylon the students of the law appeared at a young lady's wedding with their hair richly anointed in honor of the bride. At a widow's marriage the throwing about of nuts and roasted ears of wheat was omitted. Part of the same symbolism was the usage of sowing in a flower-pot, either on the wedding-day or a little time earlier, grains of barley, notoriously of such quick growth, a sportive suggestion of the fruitfulness of the new marriage. Among the Jews in the middle ages it was still usage to strew about wheat or barley in the house where the wedding took place; or else, as the ancient Persians did at their betrothals, to sprinkle the young married couple with them. In the same suggestive spirit the inhabitants of Tur Malka used to carry in front of the bridal couple chanti-cleer and one of his wives. The inhabitants of Beta were still more elaborate in their symbolic procedure; they used to plant a cedar at the birth of every boy, an acacia whenever a girl came into the world; and when young people married, cut down the birth-tree of each and use it as material for furnishing the bridal chamber.

Of anything like a priest's blessing in consecrated places, as essential to or accompanying marriage, we find no trace in the older rabbinical writings; the first trace of anything of the kind I think I have discovered in a casual observation contained in the Pirke of R. Eliazar, a work composed under Mohammedan dominion. In the biblical era, the bridal pair was blessed by the parents, relatives, and all the people present (Ruth iv. 11). In Tobias (vii. 13), the Greek text has it that Raguel blessed the newly married pair, but does not give the formula of the benediction, but the Latin translation gives it: et apprehendens dexteram filiæ suæ dextræ Tobiæ tradidit, dicens: Deus Abraham et Deus Isaac et Deus Jacob vobiscum sit et ipse conjugat vos impleatque benedictionem suam in vobis—"and laying the right hand of his daughter into the right hand of Tobias, he said: The God of Abraham, Isaac, and Jacob be with you, and join you Himself together and fulfill His promised blessing in you."

The wedding ring—which might only be of simple metal without any precious stone—was borrowed quite clearly from the Romans, among whom it was customary for the betrothed man to send his promised bride an iron ring without any stone. It cannot be shown that the Greeks ever used the ring; but it occurs among the Mohammedans. In the Christian church the ring is not mentioned as used at the wedding earlier than the tenth century; while at the betrothal in the very first Christian centuries, the young man usually tendered to his chosen, when she gave her consent, a ring of gold as a pledge and token that they were soon to be irrevocably given to each other.

The Talmud is unacquainted with the custom, evidently of later origin, according to which the bride, before the ceremony was performed, was deprived of her head of hair; a usage met with also among the Greeks. Moses Alaschkar, a learned Rabbi of the sixteenth century, warmly inveighs against this custom in an open letter addressed to Tlemesan, insisting that in Mohammedan countries Jewish women from the most ancient times carried their wealth of hair visibly and unconcealed, and that in Christian countries they conceal it not from any religious obligation, for none existed, but merely in conformity with general manners, which enjoined upon Christian married women too that they should not go about with uncovered heads.

In regard to other usages, however, all of which are directly resulting from and typify the exalted conception entertained of marriage, a difference prevailed between the inhabitants of Judea and Galilee; as an instance may be given that in Judea the bridal couple were permitted a private interview of one hour's duration before the final performance of the marriage ceremony, while the Galileans allowed no such thing.

There was great merriment at the wedding. Everything was done that dancing and music could do to make the guests as happy as possible. A sort of orchestra was formed out of all kinds of the most incongruous instruments, flutes, harps, zithers, castagnets; tambourines were a very important item in these instrumental musical resources which were now and then helped out by clappings of hands, and occasionally varied by cheerful singing which often attracted a great crowd of people. It was a popular saying that when the castagnet was heard the matron of sixty was as ready to run to the sound as the girl of six. Now and then the tide of merriment when at its height— and the most serious among the guests threw gravity aside and helped to swell it—was checked by some one present delivering a short speech of moral reflections. Moderation, indeed, was especially enjoined by the moral teachers in respect of outbursts of joy and merriment at weddings. R. Ashe, observing at the marriage of his own son that the students were losing self-command almost in their boisterous humor, deliberately threw a valuable vase to the ground in order to stem the overflowing current of hilarity. R. Hamnuna the Less, once pressed to sing at a marriage banquet, broke out with the strain, " Woe to us we must die, woe to us we must die !" whereupon the others responded in chorus, "Bless the truth, bless the law, which are our guard and defense." One of the sages also compared the transitory joys of life with the momentary pleasures of a marriage feast. The later Rabbis, who were just as little able to conceive of a wedding without its music, would not have anything sung on the occasion save religious hymns, and prohibited dancing altogether, founding their opposition on the passage of Proverbs (xi. 21), "Hand in hand remains not wholly pure."

Invitations to a wedding banquet were regarded as a special mark of respect. The Jews of Jerusalem had a peculiarity as to this, evincing great reserve and distinction of manners; it was not usual there to go to such a celebration unless the invitations for the family had been numerous and pressing. On the other hand, if any one who might fairly expect an invitation was overlooked, he was justly offended, and now and then took occasion to make the uncourteous giver of the feast feel that he was offended. R. Jehuda Hanasi, for instance, invited to the wedding of his son, R. Simon, all the learned men, and only left out Bar Kappara, disliking and fearing his sarcastic tongue. Whereupon Bar Kappara wrote on the wall of the house where the wedding was to be celebrated: "240 million denars are to be spent on this feast—and Bar Kappara is not invited! If such luxury falls to the lot of sinners, what grandeur will not pious people have some day!" The consequence of this was, that he had an invitation sent him, and then he altered the last sentence and said, "If the pious have the enjoyment of such splendors even in this life, what glories must be reserved for them in the other!" According to another authority, Bar Kappara's vengeance was of a more elaborate and witty sort than what we have given. He wrote on the door of R. Jehuda's house: "Death follows thy joys, what are thy joys worth?" After R. Jehuda had found out who the writer was, he had guests invited to a special banquet prepared for him for the following day. Hardly had the dishes been put on the table, when Bar Kappara began to pour out a whole litany of ridiculous stories about foxes, and the guests became so absorbed in his proceedings that they paid no attention to the delicacies before them until they were quite spoiled and had to be taken back to the kitchen untasted. The liberal host could not help complaining a little about it to Bar Kappara, but received from him this answer: "I did it because you did not invite me with my colleagues, and also that you might not run away with the idea that I was enamored of your good cookery."

At the wedding banquet the bridegroom took the most prominent seat, while it was one of the conventional duties of the bride to keep in the background with maidenly modesty, and it was regarded as a duty of the guests to give all the pleasure they could to the groom and his young partner, in everything they said and did. Friends testified their sympathy for the bridegroom by wedding presents, which were not of arbitrary choice, but had to be selected according to certain rules distinctly prescribed by law; the groom for his part sent all sorts of love-gifts to his bride. He led the procession on horse-back, and so, bearing all sorts of vessels of wine and oil, gold and silver caskets, silk garments, and other articles, it proceeded to the house of his bride's parents, before the door of which he held out the wine-cup, which was there filled for him to drink—a sort of loving-cup. The bridal-chamber was furnished in the most luxurious manner; linens of divers colors, stuffs of silk and purple, ornaments of pure gold, and fruits of every sort and description adorned its walls.

In the times of mediæval oppression, when barbarous persecutors forbade the practice of their religion to the Jewish people, there were many reasons why Jewish parents should keep as secret as possible the occasions when the distinctive

Jewish rites attending infancy, and especially when weddings were performed. Accordingly friends of the faith had to be notified when such celebrations were to happen by secret signs and tokens. The Talmud says, " When the screaming sound of the hand-mill is heard in a large building, this signifies that a circumcision feast is coming off; when the windows of a house in Berur-Chajil are brilliantly illuminated, it was understood that people were invited to a wedding."

According to old-biblical usage, the marriage festival lasted a full week. On the Saturday following the wedding-day, the bridegroom was distinguished in several ways in public worship, and was still looked upon as the hero of the day. The origin of this usage is in Rabbinical books thus described. When King Solomon built the temple, he had two doors prepared; these were to be regarded as places specially consecrated to the spirit of kindness in man; one was called the Bridegroom's door, the other the Mourner's. On Saturdays the crowd used to gather before these doors, to see who would enter at them. When one went through the bridegroom's door, they called to him, " May God, whose throne is in this house, rejoice thee with sons and daughters." The mourners then came up to pass through the other door, and the usual cry to them was, " May the Owner of this house comfort ye ; " then followed those excommunicate who were thus addressed, " The Lord soften your hearts that ye yield to authority, and the congregation reckon ye as of it again." After the destruction of the Temple, the Rabbis instituted the practice that every bridegroom and every mourner should visit the synagogue or the lecture hall, in order that the people, always numerous there, might have an opportunity of rejoicing with the one and consoling the other.

So much, briefly, concerning the marriage customs of the time for which the Talmud and Midraschim must be regarded as our authorities. We see already that, original and native as all these are in the main, foreign elements have crept in, and the influence of neighboring peoples is unmistakably there. The same impression and to a much greater degree comes irresistibly into the mind of the archæologian when he examines the marriage customs of the later centuries up to our own time. We have already remarked above, that the Spanish and French Jews had tournaments at their weddings; the Sicilian and Arabian Jews, torchlight processions; and in what follows we shall meet with many a custom which never grew up on purely Jewish soil, many a one which, after becoming accredited among the people, had to be eliminated and put down as intrusive and foreign and repugnant to religion by the Rabbis.

We commence our delineation of marriage among the later Jews with a country respecting whose Jewish inhabitants, notwithstanding the early date of their settlement in it, the investigator is supplied with but scanty material—western and southern India. From about the close of the fifth century, Jews in considerable numbers, under the stress of the persecution set on foot by the Persian King Firuz, had repaired to Malabar, Ceylon, Cochin, for a new home, and there formed themselves into independent religious congregations, with free privilege to live and worship, and the Jews still to be found in these parts of India and adjacent countries can be no other than descendants of these early settlers. Singular good fortune has preserved for us liturgical forms used by the Cingalese Jews, which were sent by Iecheskel, Rabbi of Cochin on the Malabar coast, to a certain Tobias Boas at the Hague—Ceylon was, it should be noted, Dutch

territory at the time—and printed about a century ago in
Amsterdam. This liturgical book gives a full and particular
statement of the marriage ceremonies among Cingalese Jews,
which covers several successive pages. Many of the details
are more fully explained by a translation into the vernacular
speech, probably an Indian dialect. That this liturgy as a
whole dates from a very early period, when Cingalese Jews
were under rulers or head-men of their own race, appears from
a strophe of a song contained in it.

What strikes us immediately and unmistakably here at the
first glance is that the Cingalese Jews were to all intents and
purposes Rabbinical in their religious foundation. Marriage
festivals are celebrated for a space of seven days; the bride
bathes in a bath of Rabbinical prescription; there are the bridesmaids, and seven blessings, there is the marriage deed, Kethubah,
and the peculiar form and method of pronouncing the benediction. Everything testifies to the influence of Talmudic dis-
quisition and precept. The observance of the seven days is
carried out in the severest and most consequent manner.
There are separate observances and songs assigned to each of
these days. Songs for female voices, music of other kinds
abounded in the festivities, and wax tapers were lavishly used.
There was one usage peculiar to them alone; the bride was on
the Monday night bathed, and then escorted to the sound
of tambourines to the house where the wedding was celebrated; the roll of the law was opened, while she stood close
by, at the ten commandments, to which she reverentially
put her lips, while the Rabbi pronounced over her a special
benediction made up of pointed passages from the Bible   On
Tuesday the guests assembled at the house where the wedding

festival is going on, the bridegroom placed gold and silver articles in some vessel, which was then placed on the fire and the contents fused into one mass. The old men made a solemn examination of this mass of alloy, while the women vented their feeling in concerted song. The groom and his "best men" then dressed themselves in a handsome manner and sat down to a banquet, during which strains of various kinds were sung to them. On the evening of the same day the bridegroom, with his person all concealed by white festive garments, attended by his groomsmen similarly clad, was led into the synagogue to the sound of tambourines; and thence escorted back by the whole congregation to the bride's house, with four large wax tapers being borne in front of the whole party. On the way all sorts of songs were sung. Having reached the bridal house, they led the bride to a chair specially prepared for her, and covered her with a thick vail. The bridegroom took a place directly opposite her, his hand holding a cup filled with wine, whereto the wedding ring was tied by some fastening. There-upon a dialogue in a sort of recitative began between bride-groom and congregation, at the close of which the bridegroom spoke the specific formula which effects the union in wedlock, and put the ring upon the bride's finger. The Rabbi then read out loud the Kethuba, and held a catechetical dialogue with the bridegroom as to the obligations incurred in marriage. The bridegroom signed the Kethuba, two witnesses also attesting the fact with their signatures, and handed it, pronouncing a special formula, to the bride, who was then unvailed by the women, singing a song while they did it, and placed by them on a couch. The Rabbi spoke the seven blessings, the congregation recited appointed songs, then led the bridegroom solemnly to the bride and retired, after uttering all sorts of wishes for their happiness. Next night—that of Thursday—and on the following nights the guests assembled at the house of the wedding, and sang special songs for each night as they sat at supper. On the last night, finally, the young couple were escorted with music by men and women to the house of God, where the bridegroom himself led in the evening prayer, and then returned with the whole cortége to his dwelling, where the close of the festival was solemnized by an assemblage of guests and the singing of cheerful songs.

Maimoni makes it a reproach to the Jews of Egypt, and considers it a very mischievous circumstance, that in their weddings they comply with strange un-Jewish usages, and even perform a sort of mummery. The bride covers her head with a helmet, takes a sword in her hand, and so travestied, dances at the head of the procession of the marriage guests. The bridegroom then allows himself to be dressed up in women's garments by persons of that sex, skilled in matters of the toilet, female clothing is put on the boys who are present, and their nails stained with henna. Maimoni's narrative informs us that, although men of distinction in Egypt clung with great pertinacity to these usages, and the people in particular had become deeply attached to them from habit, he succeeded, in spite of this, in bringing about their complete extirpation.

Concerning marriage ceremonies in Bagdad, Persia, and Northern Africa, we have information from "Benjamin"— whose statements, however, are to be used with great circumspection—in the work which he entitles his "Journeys." (Eight Years in Asia and Africa, pp. 111, 112; 269–270; 276, 277.) In a general way the usages which he reports bear a certain

5

affinity to the marriage ceremonies peculiar to Oriental peoples.

The marriage usages of the Jews in European countries, so far as our available sources of information enable us to judge, do not differ materially. That here and there national and non-Jewish customs should and did creep even into the synagogue is easily intelligible; the differences we do find are principally of a liturgical kind. Of such liturgical specialties Abudraham in his work mentions some as peculiar to the congregations of Seville, Toledo, and other Spanish cities. The marriage ceremonies of the German Jews in the middle ages are described by R. Eleazar b. Jehuda of Worms. One very striking circumstance is, that they were in the habit of solemnizing marriage on the day dedicated to the Teutonic Venus, Freia, Friday.* When the bride solemnly enters the bridegroom's house, he meets her at the threshold, takes her hand and lays it on the lintel of the house door, probably for the same reason for which the Romans used to hand the keys of the house to the bride at the moment when the bridesmaids lifted her over the threshold, to signify that she was mistress of that house. After the marriage ceremony, the bridal pair sat

---

* The translator cannot forbear remarking that the writer of this essay is in error when he represents Freia as the analogue of the Latin Venus. Had she been so, it would scarcely have happened that Hebrews would have adopted her day for their weddings, on the contrary, they would have carefully avoided it. The Latin "Venus" is physical in her attributes chiefly, though not exclusively. The Teutonic "Freia," on the contrary, represents all that is at once ideal and legitimate in love and marriage. But in the Christian middle ages it is very little probable that her attributes or herself were much remembered by any Germans, save perhaps by those of the peasant class, among whom antique heathendom has preserved a feeble cryptic existence throughout the centuries.

down to a special meal, principally composed of honey and cheese, the motive of which was the proverbial speech, "honey and milk are under thy tongue." Besides the fruit-seeds, salt too was strewn about in the house where the marriage was performed, to characterize symbolically the covenant that was entered into as one that was to last for eternity, and from which there could never be release. On the Sunday following the wedding day, the newly married man delivered, on the very instant of his return home from synagogue, to his young spouse his cloak, girdle, and hat, by way of open recognition that she was henceforth a sharer in all that was his. Of the betrothals and weddings of the Jews of Frankfort Schudt discourses in his " Jüdische Merkwürdigkeiten," throwing carelessly together old things and new after his fashion. Concerning the usages of the Jews of Rhineland, in particular of Mayence, we have full information from Maharil in his Minhagim. What is to be especially noticed in regard to these, is that the marriage ceremony of a virgin bride was performed in the synagogue on the Bimah, that of a widow in the outer court of the temple. No particular stress is laid on the reading of the marriage deed, the Kethuba. In the Kol Bo it is required that the Kethuba should be translated into the vernacular.

As to marriage among the Karaites, it is to be observed that, as was the case generally with their whole doctrinal system, many rabbinical elements, however forbidden, got in one way or another. Speaking generally, it differs but little from the common forms of marriage in vogue among the Oriental Jews. Ashes were strewn on the heads of the bridal couple, to commemorate the destruction of Jerusalem. The seven blessings were adopted without alteration, and supplemented by numerous passages from the Bible. The already mentioned formula of the seven benedictions occurs among them also. The bridesmaids and groomsmen (paranymphs) are mentioned both in the liturgy and in many songs. The Kethuba, or, as the Karaites call it, Sh'tar, was composed in Hebrew. Among other things the married pair bound themselves expressly in it, if they ever should reach the holy land, conscientiously to keep the Jewish festivals according to antique usage, viz.: by carefully observing the changes of the moon.

The marriages of Jews of quite recent times have only this one peculiarity that need engage attention, that instead of the old tone of natural and religious joy which sprang from the heart, we now too often see the stiff etiquette of the *salon*, and it is only in a few localities that the old forms, artless and happy as they were, have held their ground against the general tendency to sublimate and refine away what antiquity has handed down. Particularly interesting in this connection is the account from the pen of a French tourist, of a Jewish marriage celebrated not long ago in Alsatia. Here we see the "Mashaliks," who have so long disappeared from our weddings, still amusing the guests with their improvised discourses, abounding in surprising turns and twists of thought; the costumes, so singular and of such venerable antiquity, defy the universal supremacy of French fashion, and the man of the world from Paris who witnesses and reports the scene, tells us that he could not help fancying that he sat at table with ghosts that had risen straight out of the grave of the preceding century.

ON

INTERMENT OF THE DEAD.

IN POST-BIBLICAL JUDAISM.

A Study in Archæology.

By Dr. JOSEPH PERLES.

On Interment of the Dead

IN POST-BIBLICAL JUDAISM.

A STUDY IN ARCHÆOLOGY.

By Dr. JOSEPH PERLES.

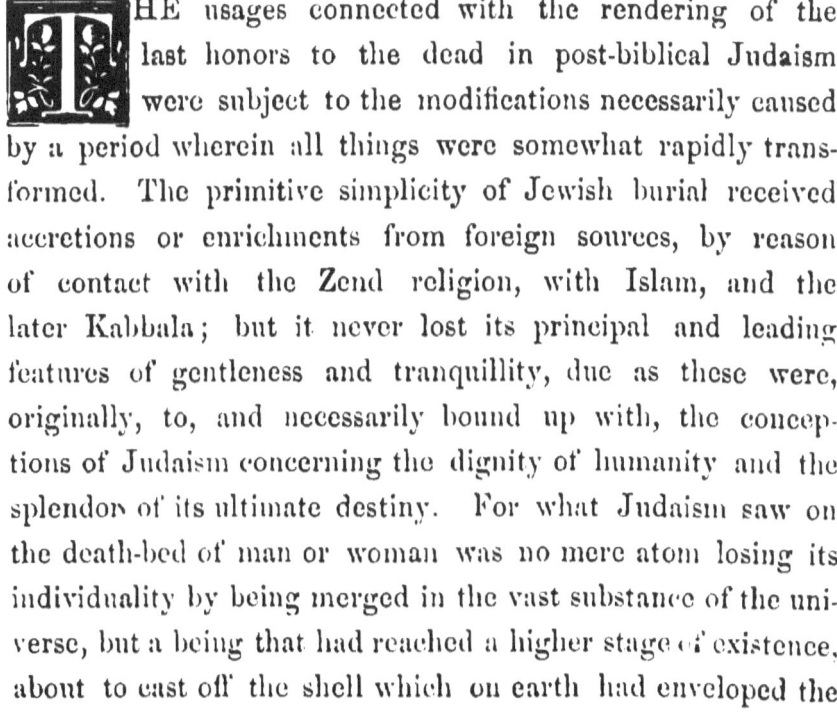

HE usages connected with the rendering of the last honors to the dead in post-biblical Judaism were subject to the modifications necessarily caused by a period wherein all things were somewhat rapidly transformed. The primitive simplicity of Jewish burial received accretions or enrichments from foreign sources, by reason of contact with the Zend religion, with Islam, and the later Kabbala; but it never lost its principal and leading features of gentleness and tranquillity, due as these were, originally, to, and necessarily bound up with, the conceptions of Judaism concerning the dignity of humanity and the splendor of its ultimate destiny. For what Judaism saw on the death-bed of man or woman was no mere atom losing its individuality by being merged in the vast substance of the universe, but a being that had reached a higher stage of existence, about to cast off the shell which on earth had enveloped the

imperishable soul, and to enter on the pure sphere of the spirit-
ual life.   Hence, originally, mourning for the dead was carefully
kept within bounds, and the leading feature of observance was
the bestowal of solemn and anxious care in the disposition of
the corpse, so lately the vessel wherein the immortal part was
contained ; while the departed spirit itself was, so to speak, left
alone and undisturbed to its peace and rest.   It was not until
a later time, when the masses for the dead of the Christian
Church, and the sensuous notions of the Koran and the Kabbala,
began to have their influence on Judaism, that prayers for the
dead and other foreign usages accompanied obtrusively the
flight of the spirit to the world beyond.   But the corpse was an
object of devout and tender respect only because it was thought
that between it and the soul that had taken wing some continu-
ing relation needs must be, because the Hebrew mind was
possessed by the poetic thought that this world and the world
to come held out, as it were, arms to embrace each other, and
that they even had lips which could meet with a parting kiss.
Hence, it was thought that the separation of the two elements
of earthly existence, body and soul, could not be sudden and
abrupt, but that the latter still for some days hovered and lin-
gered around the mansion which had sheltered it so long, taking
its final departure only then when Death had begun to set his
seal irrevocably and certainly on his work in the visible marks of
corruption.   It resulted from such ideas that any desecration
of the grave, such as the Parsees were wont to practice in their
detestation of physical interment, was regarded by Hebrews with
horror and aversion as profanity to the dead, and a wicked
disturbance of the " eternal sleep" (Jerem. li. 39, 57); while,
on the other hand, complete preservation of the physical frame

by embalmment or other means, as in vogue among Egyptians and other peoples, was carefully avoided. Embalmment, it is possible, may have been employed on very rare occasions, and in the case of some few highly distinguished personages, and there are some other alleged cases of preservation of the corpse by such methods; but these are either to be regarded as exceptional, or, more probably, to be considered as belonging to fable and legend alone. We are told, for example, that the corpse of Eleazar ben Simon was kept by his wife, according to his injunction, more than twenty years, in the garret of his house; but the reason of this is expressly given, because he did not wish to be submitted to the discourteous or disrespectful mode of interment intended for him by his hostile and embittered fellow-teacher; while the stories that Herod kept the corpse of a girl preserved seven years long in honey, and that Chija ben Abuhu kept the skull of King Joiachin wrapped up in silk in a bureau, bear their legendary character unmistakably upon their face.

That some solemn disposition of the mortal remains should be made was so natural and inevitable a claim of human feeling, that, originally and at the outset, man saw no need of seeking for it the sanction of religious law or of considering it as founded in scriptural injunction. It was only at a later time, when the Jewish religion was at best but tolerated by the side of that of Zoroaster, that the necessity was felt in Jewish circles of entering into a formal justification of their own practice of burial, so precious to themselves, so detested by their opponents. King Sapor asks R. Chama to give him passages from the Bible supporting the practice of consigning bodies to the earth; and in consequence of this request the Jewish doctors of the law pro-

posed to themselves the question, what was the leading motive
of burial; whether the feeling so prevalent among most of the
peoples of antiquity, that there was dishonor and shame in per-
mitting the corpse to putrefy above the earth ; or rather that the
corpse ought to be returned to the bosom of mother earth, in
some sort, for purification from earthly offense. According
as this question is decided one way or the other, practice will
differ in the ritual of interment; but the underlying moral
thought connected with the practice is in no way affected by the
answer. The second view supports the well-known preference
for interment in the Holy Land, to whose soil was attributed
a specially atoning power ; while it was the first view that led
the Rabbis in Jamnia to insert in the liturgy a special form of
praise and blessing commemorative of the interment, happily
after difficulty brought about, of those who had fallen on the
day of Betar.* So highly was this pious observance, indeed,
esteemed in the Jewish world, that the Agadists even referred
the passage of the Bible, " Abraham gave all that was his to
Isaac," to the place of burial which he left to be hereditary for
the family. In all the towns there were, at certain places,
special subscription-boxes for burial expenses, and every one
who remained for nine months in the locality was under the
duty of contributing.

To comprehend aright the spirit of noble resignation which
is embodied in Jewish funeral ceremonials, it must be remembered that, according to the apprehension of the Jewish sages,

---

* The fall of that fortress (135 C. E.) put a terrible end to the rising of the
Jews, led by Bar Cochba, against Roman tyranny ; it is said that more than half
a million of the devoted race either lost their lives or were sold into slavery at
that catastrophe.

this world is to be compared to a dwelling in which man is received as a temporary guest, while the passage to the life beyond was always regarded as leading to the abode of everlasting peace, and that life itself as to be passed in the house of eternity; for it was by that expressive name that, following herein the Egyptians, they called "God's acre," or the burial place, where, according to the expression of the Psalmist, those who have reached their last home find their everlasting mansion in the grave. To disturb the rest of this second home was regarded as a proof of the most extreme hardness of heart, and the barbarous conduct of the Parsees, who in their fanaticism tore the corpses even of strangers to their faith from their graves that they might be devoured, according to Parsee usage, by birds of prey, drew many a cry of anguish from Jewish breasts. "Sink my coffin deep, deep into the earth," says dying Jose b. Kisma to his disciples, "for a Parsee horse is haltered to every date-palm of Babylon, and there is no coffin in Palestine out of which some Median charger does not feed as from a manger." "Let my burial-clothes be but scanty," is the last injunction of R. Chiskija, "and let the grave be deep that receives my coffin." And Simeon b. Jochai exclaims, "When thou seest the steed of a Zoroastrian trampling graves in the soil of Holy Land, know that our miseries have reached their climax, and expect at any moment Messiah's hour!" And Rabba b. Samuel is of opinion that the threat in the Book of Samuel (i. 12, 15), that "God's chastisement will strike ye and your forefathers," was visibly fulfilled in the desecration of Jewish corpses by Parsees.

After these prefatory remarks we now proceed to deal particularly with our special subject.

The dying person wrestles, as it were, with Death. This last agony must not be aggravated by outcries and lamentations of those around the bed of death, nor may the release of the body from its final trial be accelerated one instant by the slightest touch. The death that sets it free approaches at last in the form of the Angel of Death, represented in imagination and fable as a being almost entirely made up of widely-opened eyes, and as standing during the last moments of life at the head of the dying creature with a drawn sword in his hand. On the point of the sword there is a drop of gall, at the sight of which the dying person opens the mouth in terror; death comes at the very instant that he swallows this drop of gall, and this drop it is, also, which works a little later that alteration of the countenance that follows death. Those who have been present at the death-struggle then tear their clothes. After the breath has departed the eyes are closed, usually by the eldest son, the fallen jaw is raised and the mouth bound up, the corpse itself bathed, anointed, and, in order to check too rapid corruption, covered with vessels of metal or glass, or else with salt, and deposited on bare earth, or on a layer of refrigerative salt.

As now among Jews, so of old; in this respect, that few were regarded as endowed with sufficient tact and intelligence to perform the delicate task of bearing news of a death to those concerned. The inhabitants of Sepphoris threatened death to any one who should bring them news of the dissolution of R. Jehuda Hanasi. Bar Kappara undertook to do it, but conveyed the intelligence in figurative language. He appeared before them with covered head and torn garments, and lifted up his voice in lamentation. "The angels above and the mighty men here have had a struggle for the possession of the tablets of the law, the angels have carried off the victory, and borne away the tablets!" "Rabbi is dead," interrupted the Seppho-ræans. "It is ye who have said it," answered Bar Kappara with a gesture of assent, "not I."

Popular belief loved to dignify the death of special favorites or of the specially illustrious by miraculous narratives, or else to bring real events into some sort of connection with their last moments. When R. Acha died, says the legend, stars were visible in the clear light of noon; when R. Chanina of Bath-Hauran died, the sea of Tiberias divided itself like the Red Sea of old; at the death of R. Samuel b. Yizchak, a storm tore up the cedars of Palestine by the roots; at that of R. Jose b. Chalafta, streams of blood flowed through the streets of Lydda; when R. Jose was torn away from the world, the citadel of Tiberias fell with a crash; on the death-day of R. Chija meteoric stones fell abundantly from the sky; on that of R. Hamnuna, hail-storms devastated the neighbor-hood far and wide; in the year of the death of R. Meshar-shija, thorns grew out of the date-palms; and when R. Abuhu went to his last home, the very pillars in the buildings of Cæsarea could not refrain from tears.

The precepts of religion enjoined that bursts of grief for the dead should be as much as possible restrained and moderated, and that mourning for them should not take exaggerated forms; but natural impulse and the contagious example of neighbor-peoples in this respect sometimes prevented the voice of reason from being heard. R. Akiba, coming quite abruptly upon the procession carrying R. Eliesar b. Kisri to the grave, was moved to scourge his own body till the blood flowed; and R. Hamnuna found it necessary to remind once more the women of his time that it was a forbidden thing to tear out their hair when one dear to them had died.

When one died, the news was proclaimed abroad to the sound of a trumpet; and the public, where the death had occurred, participated in the mourning, for all the inhabitants of the locality refrained, though probably only for a very brief time, from their usual labors. But in the case of men of distinction, the mourning was far more extensive. When a teacher of the law died, his school was closed; when the Ab-beth-din died, instruction ceased for a while, as of course, in all the schoolhouses of the city; when the Nasi died, it was the same with all the schools of the State.

Between death and interment there was but a short interval. It was a special privilege or attribute of the city of Jerusalem that no corpse was permitted to pass a night within its walls. The cruelty of such quick burial was more apparent than real, for it was mitigated by the circumstance that, as we shall see later, the corpses were deposited in open graves, and carefully inspected for several days, to provide for the rare case when death had not really occurred. It is a very one-sided interpretation of the law that finds in this usage any warrant or justification for the very altered circumstances of subsequent times. Bachya ben Ascher and Chaskuni declare expressly that it was applicable only in Palestine itself; while Menasseh ben Israel, who, in spite of his extensive general culture, was still controlled by many prejudices, pronounces for its unqualified retention.

In this interval measures were taken preparatory to the actual consignment to earth. The dead body was bathed and

˙anointed, on which occasion drugs and spices of the most various kinds were employed in the most abundant measure; myrtle, aloes; later, also hyssop, oil of roses, and rose-water, with
carefully prescribed ceremonies and forms of prayer. Great
stress was laid on the point of bathing the corpse; and it is
related, in pity or in accusation, of the Babylonians (probably
the Jews of Babylon) that their dead go to the grave without
due honor, with no torch-light procession, and even unbathed.

The body thus bathed and anointed, was wrapped in garments specially appropriated to the corpse. To be consigned
naked to the grave was thought, among Jews as among many
other peoples, dishonor and shame; and the connections of the
deceased considered it a meritorious thing and expressive of
the extent of their grief, to put a quantity of valuable garments
upon the mortal remains; in this proceeding they were usually
a little hampered by the remonstrances of sensible friends, for
the garments which had once touched the corpse could never
be used afterwards for any other purpose. There was so
much expense and display in this matter of dressing corpses,
that, as the Talmud drastically puts it, the interment of the
corpse was frequently a more serious matter to relatives than
the death itself, and that many who could not stand the enormous cost, and yet did not like not to conform to existing
usage, solved the matter by abandoning their homes, leaving
the corpses of their relatives to such interment as the town
would bestow. In order to put some check on these abuses,
R. Gamaliel left orders that he should be buried only in linen
garments. This good example was not without its effect, and
in R. Papa's times people had got so far as to not to feel any hesita-
tion about wrapping a corpse in an overcoat which only cost a

sus.* R. Chiskija also warmly opposed the practice of heaping a mass of garments upon corpses, and we are told that he was interred in a simple linen cloth. It was customary also to use the worn-out wrappings of the rolls of the law, which could not lawfully be applied to any ordinary purpose, for burial garments. As regards the color of these costumes of the dead, usage differed greatly. R. Josia wished to be consigned to earth in white robes. R. Jannai said before his death to his sons: " Wrap me neither in white nor black garments, for I would not appear as a mourner among the joyous, or as joyous among mourners, but put me parti-colored garments on." R. Jochanan uttered a similar request. R. Jirmija's desire was to be wrapped in a white stuff weaved of prickly plants, with shoes on his feet and a staff in his hand, and to be laid on his side, in order that he might be completely prepared for the resurrection. In the middle ages red burial-clothes were in vogue as well as white.

Kings wished their very burial costume to bear witness to their departed grandeur. Accordingly Herod was borne to the grave on a golden bier inlaid with a great number of precious stones. The pall and the burial-garments were of Tyrian purple. On his head the golden crown was fastened above the diadem, and in the immovable right hand was seen the royal sceptre.

The face of the corpse was originally covered and concealed only in those cases where the features were distorted, but later, in the case of all, with the single exception only of a man betrothed to marry. The corpse lay in the coffin with face turned upwards, with the hands folded on the breast, and legs

---

* The name of a small coin.

stretched out to their full length. Universal usage among the
Jews rejected any oblique attitude for the corpse, or a sitting
one, or one in which the limbs were gathered together as of one
cowering. It would appear that, as a rule, the hair was cut
from the head, and it is so expressly stated in the case of the
betrothed girl. It was not unusual with women to bequeath
their hair, by way of legacy, to designated persons.

Besides their garments, it was customary to give the dead, or
hang on their coffin, borrowing herein custom from the neighboring peoples, divers objects which they had used in life; such
as their inkstand, their writing-pen, their writing-table, their
keys. This usage was especially observed in the case of those
who died betrothed or childless. It appears to have been a
special or exclusive practice of the royal family, to deposit large
sums of money or valuable ornaments in the grave with the
dead. Thus, Herod buried the murdered Aristobulus with
particularly fine spices and other exceptionally valuable things.
Hyrcanus opened the grave of David and robbed it of three
thousand silver talents. Herod, who tried the same thing a
second time, found no money, but gold ornaments of remarkable
beauty and value.

The coffin in which the dead was consigned to earth was
either of wood, most frequently cedar, or of stone. The kind
of coffin most frequently in use was made of separate planks.
The coffin of bronze in which, according to legend, the Egyptians
sank Joseph's corpse in the Nile, or deposited it, according to
another version, in the labyrinth, is suggestive of Egyptian
rather than Jewish circumstances. To bury in a simple matting
of reeds was regarded as dishonoring the body, and involved, in
popular belief, the consequence that the soul of one who had
6

received such sepulture could never extricate itself from the
tomb and join the multitudinous company of invisible spirits
who were always traversing the world. It has been already
remarked that the coffin was decorated with all sorts of ornaments, emblems, crowns or garlands. On the coffin of distinguished scholars, like R. Huna, and of pious kings eminent
for service to the community, like Chiskija, a roll of the law
was deposited, to illustrate the zeal wherewith the dead had
prosecuted either the study or the application of the truths of
religion. This custom was modified later, and the roll of the
law merely carried in front of the bier to the grave. On the
coffin of one who died excommunicate, the supreme court of
law appointed a person to deposit a stone in token of expiation.
The Rabbis of the middle ages, however, regarded death as a
complete purgation of the sentence of excommunication, and,
accordingly, abolished entirely the Talmudic custom of depos-
iting the stone. Above the coffin of those who died betrothed,
canopies profusely decorated were raised; and, generally, the
interment of such persons was marked by the special honor of
lavish expenditure and ornament. The coffin was also frequently crowned with garlands of myrtle twigs; and incense,
originally but sparingly or exceptionally employed, was later,
in the case of persons of rank, used customarily, with the most
lavish unrestraint. A sort of libation of honor, on the bier of the
dead, may have been practiced occasionally. The French Jews
of the middle ages were in the habit of having their coffins made
from the table which had borne testimony in life to their
generous hospitality. In Spain, and particularly in Gerona,
according to the statement of R. Nissim ben Reuben, coffins
were gradually disused, and the dead body, without any other

envelope, consigned to its last resting-place in earth. This custom, which is of mystical significance, has maintained itself even to the present day.

The burial procession, which went from the house of the departed to the cemetery—God's acre, so called—was the object of careful attention and special care. Pains were taken to have as many as possible take part in it. Everybody who met it on its way, was in duty bound to join and accompany it to the grave. Even the study of the law, on which such store was set, was to be interrupted in order to pay these last honors to the dead. At all points where the procession passed spectators rose from their seats, as a mark of respect to the dead, or, as others explain, to the company bound on this errand of grief. According to the views of the ancients, the procession to the grave was adequate and satisfactory only in the case where it extended itself, at least espalier-wise, from the very house of mourning to the place of sepulture itself, by such additions. But when it is computed that sometimes the numbers of those who thus of duty and obligation joined in its passage to the grave, mounted up even to many thousands, this must surely be no more than somewhat sportive hyperbole.

The mode of carrying the corpse was dependent upon the age of the deceased person. Children who died before the end of their first month, and who were still regarded as mere embryos, were taken without any special ceremony of mourning to a burial-place, as it would seem, specially reserved for such cases. Children of more than a month were carried to their resting-place in a coffin under the arm; those who had lived more than one full year, on a bier carried on men's shoulders. In the case of grown-up people, a distinction was originally made between people of large or slender means, the former being conveyed in a carriage, the latter on a simple bier; at a later day, the carriage was used without exception for all alike ; the bier, which in the great majority of instances was of wood, in the case of persons of very high rank, of precious metal highly chased and decorated in the richest manner.

There is a legend that King Chiskija caused his father to be carried to the grave upon a very simple military or field bedstead, as a token that atonement was needed for the sinful life he had led. The bearers of the bier, who went with naked feet, were frequently changed in the passage to the grave, in order that as many as possible might share in this labor of love. For this purpose, the bier was from time to time laid down in the street or road, and the pauses before the procession resumed its course were filled up with songs of lamentation. But there were certain days when such interruptions of the passage to the grave were not permitted in the case of male corpses, and they were never practiced or permissible in the case of female dead. The bier on which the dead was carried made a line of division between the two sexes. In some localities, the men preceded, the women followed the bier, as was Greek custom; in others, the inverse order was observed.

The interment of crowned heads and persons of the most exalted social position was exceptional in regard to many observances exclusively practiced in their honor. Any objects, as furniture and the like, of which they had made marked and favorite use, were burned; a custom expressly stated to have been borrowed from the neighboring peoples; their riding horses were hamstrung, and there were other similar observances. In honor of the deceased R. Gamaliel the elder, the

famous convert Onkelos erected a funeral pyre the cost of
which amounted to nearly seventy Tyrian minæ. And in all
other possible respects, the sepulture of kings was performed
with extraordinary solemnity and splendor. At the burial of
King Chiskija, we are told that many thousand soldiers, it is even
stated thirty-six thousand, were marshaled in the fullest military
array, and the whole distance from the house of mourning where
he died, to the hereditary burial-place of the Davidian family,
was covered with carpet. The expensively decorated coffin of
Herod was, according to the description of the interment given
by Josephus, carried by the sons and nearest relations ; and,
indeed, it was general usage that the connections and friends of
the departed were employed in the performance of the last ser-
vices of love. These coffin-bearers, in Herod's case, were
followed by military detachments representing the various regi-
ments and nationalities in the service, in complete equipment
and under the command of the generals and centurions. The
closing part of the procession was made up of five hundred attend-
ants, all carrying burning incense. At the interment of a
member of the royal family, the king in person but very rarely
attended the funeral cortége ; as a rule, on such occasions he
withdrew into strict seclusion in his own private apartments.

One of the most indispensable elements of the cortége was
composed of the Næniæ or funeral dirges of hired mourners
accomplished in such art ; to say nothing of the torch-bearers,
and the music of drums and flutes, in the arrangement of which
pains were taken, that the solemnity of the occasion should be
well marked. The function of paid mourner or singer of songs
of lamentation does not appear, however, to have been exclusively performed, as among the Romans, by a woman, known as

the *præfica ;* on the contrary, we often find such a mourner of
the male sex employed, who had a special Hebrew name. The
legal minimum of vocal and instrumental music in funeral ceremonies was composed of two flutes and a singing woman. In
Galilee, the people employed for this lamentation in music went
in front of the bier ; in Judea, behind it. The performances and
functions of these hired mourners were somewhat complicated.
They had to make solemn appeal to those present to show
signs of grief, and utter elaborate lyrical panegyrics of the dead,
beating their breasts, and expressing grief in rythmical move-
ments of the hands and feet; and the songs of mourning were
distributed between recitative of a single voice and chorus.

Besides these songs of grief, there were funeral orations at
the grave; but the fragments of those that survive show that
these were delivered only in the case of distinguished persons ;
for others there was a set and general formula of commemoration. As to the significance to be attached to the funeral
oration, opinions were divided. Some regarded it as a consola-
tory tribute to the grief of survivors, others as a mark of
honor to the dead. In the course of time, the latter view prevailed ; and the orator at the grave, in the latest times of the
usage, tried to make of his discourse a sort of mirror reflecting
the earthly career of the deceased on earth, and forecasting his
probable destiny in the other life. Any one who sincerely
deplored in words and even tears the loss of a good man dead
might fairly, according to popular ideas, expect that his sins
would be forgiven him ; for God kept count of such tears and
stored them in the treasury of eternal memory as proofs of
human love and sympathy ; while, on the other hand, it was
thought that unsympathizing people, who only joined with

lukewarm voice in the praise of a noble man departed, deserved to be buried alive themselves. The dead person, it was fancied, hears the praise uttered in his memory as in a sort of half-sleep until the coffin-lid is nailed down over him, or until corruption sets in ; and Rab before his death urged R. Samuel b. Silath to utter an impassioned oration over his corpse ; " for," said he, " I shall assuredly be there, and hear thy words as heretofore in life."

These funeral orations were probably delivered at stopping-places of the funeral cortége, or in a separate building belonging to the family of the dead, devoted to times of special mourning among them, or at the place of sepulture, sometimes even in the synagogue. When the corpse of R. Jehuda Hanasi was taken to Beth-Shearim, the cortége had eighteen stations or stopping-places; or, as it is otherwise explained, the crowd that accompanied it stopped at eighteen synagogues in order to hear the various funeral discourses delivered at each of them. R. Scira pronounced the funeral oration over one of his disciples, and Rafrem over his own daughter-in-law in the synagogue. It seems to have been occasional usage that the relatives of the deceased themselves delivered a speech for the purpose of formally thanking the public for their sympathy and attention. When the sons of R. Akiba died, the Talmud tells us that an enormous crowd of people flocked to their interment. When the usual solemnities were ended, the grief-stricken father himself ascended the rostrum, and addressed the people as follows: " Brothers in Israel, ye must hear some words from me! Even if my sons had died exalted by betrothal and approaching wedlock, the honor ye have shown them would almost have sufficed to console me in my grief. It is not because of any merit or station of mine, that ye are all here to-day; for, assuredly, many are my equals among the people. Still ye have not forgotten that the Law of God has an abiding place in the old man's heart of hearts; and it is the doctrine, the truth, the religion I represent to which ye do homage at this hour. Verily God will requite ye abundantly. Depart in peace!"

We still possess fragments of some songs and orations. The invitation to join in the song of lamentation ran thus in Palestine: "Weep with him, all ye of heavy-laden heart!" The women of Shechanzib, the inhabitants of which locality were notorious for their jesting ways, had a special and somewhat obscure *refrain* in their songs of lamentation; as, for example, "hide yourselves, cover yourselves, ye mountains, for he was the son of those exalted on earth." More intelligible because specially applied to each person over whom they were delivered, whom we happen moreover to know, and as a rule composed in the purest Hebrew, are the funeral orations, from which we give some characteristic quotations.

An orator, Bar Kipop, declaimed as follows over R. Abina: "When the devouring flame seizes the cedars, what shall the lowly hyssop do? If leviathan be taken by the angler's hook, what have the fishes of the shallow pond to expect: if the fishing line be dropped in dashing torrents, how stands it with the waters of mere brooks?" Another speaker exclaimed over the same R. Abina: "Mourn for those who are left, and not for him who has been taken away from earth; for he has entered into his rest; it is we who are bowed and broken by sorrow." R. Lakish joined in the funeral-song for a deceased young scholar from Palestine, distinguished for mastery of traditional lore, in this wise: "Woe, woe, Palestine is poorer by a man of great mark and likelihood." R. Nachman uttered the following cry of lamentation over another meritorious teacher of the law: "Alas, the very book-case is broken!" R. Chanina died on the birthday of his first-born child, and these words were uttered over him: "Joy was changed into pain; delight and dismay met each other in the way; in the very moment of happiness, grief hastened to overtake him, and, even in his hour of favor and grace, mercy failed his life." When R. Simon b. Zebid went to his last home, R. Levi thus lamented: "Earthly possessions, when they depart from us, may be replaced, for there is a vein for the silver, a stratum whence the gold is brought to the light, iron is wrested from the earth, and the metals of bronze obtained from their stones;" but when a wise man is torn away from the world, what shall balance his loss? For "where is wisdom found, and where does insight lurk? Verily they disclose themselves not to the eye of the living man. The brothers of Joseph were startled when they found valuables unexpectedly, how much more must we be stricken with terror, when we lose inestimable treasure in one who departs from us in death." R. Lakish began the funeral discourse over R. Chija b. Ada, son of Bar Kappara's sister, with the following homily: "My lover goes down into his garden, to the beds of spices, to wander about in the garden and pluck roses. The lover is God, the Lord; the garden in which he goes about is the large wide world, in which Israel sends up its perfume like a small bed of fragrant flowers, fenced round by peace; Israel where firmly founded piety and learning flourish and put forth vast leaves whereunder to shelter from life's heats: it is this bed that the Lord seeks, and plucks the queens of the garden, the roses, the disciples of the law whose belief is their delight." At the grave of Samuel Hakaton who died childless, R. Gamaliel the elder, and R. Eleazar b. Asarja thus spoke : " Here is one over whom we ought indeed to shed tears and grieve. Kings transmit their crown to their successors, the wealthy leave their treasures to their children, but Samuel has gone to his last home, and taken with him all his glorious possessions."

The public cemetery was usually situated at least fifty ells from the city boundaries. In selecting its site, care was taken that the ground should be rocky and well drained. The manners of the people altogether forbad the erection of graves or mausolea on public roads or at cross-ways, as was so customary in Greece. But the same feeling which forbad this, led to frequent interments either in gardens or very near them; and it is more than probable that graves and tombs were planted with roses, and all sorts of flowering shrubs. Any disturbance of the quiet and peace of burial-places was carefully prevented, and special measures were taken to keep wild animals from the graves, and prevent their being ravaged by such creatures. To tread the turf of the graves was regarded as showing a want of reverent feeling to the dead. R. Jonathan did it once, and received this rebuke from R. Chija : " Rabba, do you know what the dead think when you do that? They who outrage us to-day will to-morrow be here under the sod with us."

Cemeteries, as at this day in the Orient, were favorite places of resort; for the sight of graves humbles the soul, and prayer offered among them is apt to be more intense; another motive was to evoke memories of companionship with the dead, and so hold silent and imagined discourse with departed souls. It was thus that Judah b. Tabbai, who had, as Ab-beth-din,* caused an innocent man to be unjustly put to death, made a practice of visiting the victim's grave; thus that R. Joshua, who had had a severe controversy on religious questions with the disciples of Shammai, and was subsequently convinced of the infirmity of the opinions he had maintained, went to the graves of his opponents and there solemnly confessed and recanted his errors. It was also a common thing to deliver lectures on religious subjects over the graves of persons distinguished for holiness of life, and in the case of very distinguished scholars, this was commonly done on every anniversary of their death. But it must be admitted that many superstitious notions were connected with this practice of visiting cemeteries. Though it was generally held dangerous to pass an entire night in these abodes of the dead, and those who made a practice of doing so were stamped in public opinion as almost touched in mind, yet many a charlatan and enthusiast determined at any cost to establish mysterious relations with the departed, as well as for themselves the character of skillful magicians, were wont to pay these moonlit visits to the spirits. And as churchyards generally cast a gloom over the imagination, or the imagination over them, impostors may frequently have used this twilight of the mind to vail their frauds; and it is well known that, in popular belief, dust from the grave of holy men was an approved specific against fevers.

As Islam spread, so superstition in regard to the dead and their resting-place increased among the Jews. Abulsari Sahal b. Mazliach, a Karaite of the tenth century, drew up a most solemn classified catalogue of the heathenish practices of his

* The presiding judge of the Supreme Court.

rabbanite contemporaries ; they sit on graves, spend their time
uselessly in cemeteries, pray to the dead, offer up vows to them
and say : " O Joseph of the Galileans, save me, give me children." They light torches or tapers, send up incense, and join
in dances over the graves of pious people ; and, to avert illness,
hang up votive offerings on the palm-trees in the cemeteries.
Isaac Sheshet (XIV. century) tells us expressly that the Spanish
Jews of his time followed Mohammedan usage in spending the
first seven days of the mourning at the place of sepulture of
the deceased. At Saragossa, the mourners were usually followed from the Synagogue to their house by all the people in
a crowd, in the same first seven days. On the way, a professional female mourner sang a song of lament, accompanying
herself on a sort of tambourine, and the other women joined
in clapping their hands to the rhythm.

Death was regarded as a complete leveler of all distinctions
and differences of man from man during life; for, say the
Talmudists, "be things small or be they great, they find their
way at last into the grave ;" and this feeling went so far that
the very barrier of religion fell before death, and non-Jewish
corpses were allowed to rest by the side of Jewish in a common
cemetery ; yet the line was drawn in the case of crime. This
was stigmatized even by dishonoring differences in death and
burial ; less by way of punishment for the offense than as
warning to others. The suicide received but a portion of the
funeral honors accorded to others. The apostate who had
shown himself embittered against his mother-religion was even
more sternly dealt with. A man of notorious wickedness was
not allowed to rest near those whose piety had been unques-
tionable ; though this last discrimination, when people began

to pay respect to the maxim which forbids linking the idea of evil with the dead, fell into disuse. Justice provided a separate burial place for those who perished by her decrees; but the connections of the condemned were permitted, after suitable lapse of time, to collect their bones and deposit them in the family sepulchre. In like manner, the corpses of involuntary homicides who died in the cities of refuge, might, after the death of the High-Priest, be returned to their homes; while, conversely, those who died after such offense before they fled for refuge, were held bound to do so, as it were vicariously, in death, and their corpses were carried thither. Those who fell in battle were buried on the field. Death at sea under circumstances which forbad interment was always thought of with especial horror.

The cynicism of grave-diggers was proverbial, and repaid by public contempt. "Worse than a grave-digger" was a word frequently on men's lips. But for all this a Tannaite of mark, Abba Saul, unhesitatingly adopted the occupation. How anxious and systematic was the care taken by the Jewish people that their cemeteries should be well kept and of dignified appearance, is shown by a legend according to which the nations bordering Palestine, when inducing Nebuchadnezzar to invade Palestine, drew a seductive picture of the country, telling him, among other things, that there was more splendor in the cemeteries of the Jews than in his palaces.

The practice of preparing the tomb during life, abundantly testified to in the Talmud, has been maintained up to the latest time. Originally corpses were deposited in chambers, and the skeleton was subsequently taken thence and put in a coffin. At this second sepulture, when the bones were collected, there was a solemn ceremonial on a smaller scale than at the first, with orations and other usages. Piety enjoined that the bones of the dead should be carefully handled; they were wrapped in linen cloths, or deposited in some strong suitable vessel, anointed with wine and oil, and fastened together by ligaments, like mummies in Egypt. The bones of two dead persons were on no account to be rashly mixed together; and children were not permitted to perform the task of collecting the bones of deceased parents; for this, as Zadok explained to his son Eleazer b. Zadok, might somewhat impair the reverential respect due to a parent's memory.

The graves differed in character and construction at different times. Sometimes they were vaults or pits, hypogœa, for general use, sometimes they were of masonry, with oblique corridors of niches, which might be long or short at pleasure. In order to avert any approach or profanation forbidden by the law, they were distinguished outwardly by a stone whitened by chalk, in which we are perhaps to see the first traces of the grave-stone. The edifice of stone above the grave, of which the Talmud makes mention in several places, and which we may conclude from one passage to have been hollow and probably designed as a sort of guest chamber for visitors to the tomb, appears to have been in by no means general use; at all events R. Simeon b. Gamaliel declared that pious people, whose actions in life were more important than all other memorials, did not require their graves to be thus distinguished or adorned. It was a superstructure of this kind, no doubt, the monument of white stone erected by Herod on the grave of David, and that which Simon the Maccabee put up to commemorate his father and brothers, which was composed of seven towering pyramids

of polished stone, decorated with weapons of war and profusely
carved, visible from a very great distance. Of a grave-stone
the Talmud makes no mention whatever ; but it must be remembered that in Talmudic times decoration of Jewish graves had
begun to be a pretty general practice, and it may have been
thought discreet to avoid exposing the graves of Jewish dead to
profanation by provocative and conspicuous monuments ; but it
is remarked incidentally in one passage that to read the "writing
on graves" is somewhat detrimental to memory, and this sug-
gests that the graves had epitaphs.

When a body was once solemnly interred, there was great
reluctance in transferring it, for any cause, to another grave.
But an exception was made in the case of the transfer of a
corpse to a family burial-place ; for "it is sweet to man to rest
among his fathers." When burial grounds were already quite
filled, the Gaon. R. Hai allowed an upper layer of corpses to
be deposited on those already there, provided that a layer of
earth, of at least an ell in depth, could be between them.

So much concerning the solemnities attending the disposition
of the corpse, of which we are now able to see something up to
the last clod of earth thrown into the grave. As to the mourning ceremonies that followed interment, and the usages connected therewith, form the subject of a separate study. But in
some measure to make the foregoing sketch complete, the
remarks that follow may be in place.

The assembled sympathizers formed themselves into long
files which the mourners, usually clad in black, traversed to
receive a special word from every one present. On the return
from the grave, a halt was made at different places, at least
seven, partly for the purpose of uttering praises of the dead,

partly to console the mourners, and to utter some words of thanks to the assembled people. The signal for stopping at any place was given in the formula, " Take your places, worthy friends ;" for renewing the march by the formula, " Rise up, worthy friends!" In very old times, the family of the deceased prepared a funeral feast for the public, a custom of which the Talmud knows nothing, and which, as Josephus remarks, helped to impoverish many families; for in spite of the enormous expense, no one could well escape complying with it.

American Jewish Publication Society.

NEW YORK.

President.
LEOPOLD BAMBERGER, ESQ., 243 Broadway, New York.

1st Vice-President.
BENJAMIN I. HART, ESQ., 657 Broadway, New York.

2d Vice-President.
MYER STERN, ESQ., 130 Church st., New York.

Hon. Secretary.
EDWARD MORRISON, ESQ., 52 Broadway, New York.

Treasurer.
ARNOLD TANZER, ESQ., 63 Crosby st., New York.

Directors.
LOUIS LEWENGOOD, ESQ.
REV. H. S. JACOBS.
WM. B. HACKENBURG, ESQ., Philadelphia.
HON. S. WOLF, Washington, D. C.

Publication Committee.
REV. DR. G. GOTTHEIL.
REV. DR. M. MIELZINER.
REV. DR. F. DE SOLA MENDES.
M. ELLINGER, ESQ.
REV. DR. M. JASTROW, Philadelphia.

General Agent.
SOL. WEIL, ESQ., 338 E. 30th st., New York.

Hon. Vice-Presidents.

Portland, Maine.—B. Aaronson, Esq.

Boston, Mass.—Jacob Norton, Esq.

Providence, R. I.—Henry Green, Esq.

Hartford, Ct.—Joseph Schwab, Esq.

New Haven, Ct.—M. Zunder, Esq.

Bridgeport, Ct.—Moses Klein, Esq.

Waterbury, Ct.—L. Kaiser, Esq.

Rochester, N. Y.—Elias S. Ettenheimer, Esq.

Albany, N. Y.—Hon. S. W. Rosendale.

Buffalo, N. Y.—Rev Dr. S. Falk.

Syracuse, N. Y.—Rev. Dr. B. Birkenthal.

Elmira, N. Y.—Rev. Stahl.

Rondout, N. Y.—S. Weiner, Esq.

Troy, N. Y.—Rev. Dr. Eberson.

Poughkeepsie, N. Y.—Henry Wise, Esq.

Williamsburg, L. I.—Rev. Dr. Ignatz Gross.

Schenectady, N. Y.—Rev. Jos. Glück.

Newburg, N. Y.—M. H. Hirshberg, Esq.

Plattsburg, N. Y.—Henry W. Cane, Esq.

Philadelphia, Pa.—Rev. Geo. Jacobs.

Pittsburg, Pa.—Gust. Grafner, Esq.

Pottsville, Pa.—Rev. J. Oppenheim.

Williamsport, Pa.—Rev. S. Freudenthal.

Titusville, Pa.—Isaac L. Weil, Esq.

Wilkesbarre, Pa.—Rev. H. Rubin.

Oil City, Pa.—J. Seldner, Esq.

Franklin, Pa.—A. Kleinordlinger, Esq.

Alleghany City, Pa.—E. M. Greenebaum.

Cory, Pa.—Martin Stork, Esq.

Scranton, Pa.—Siegfried Sutto, Esq.

Lancaster, Pa.—Philip C. Noot, Esq.

Danville, Pa.—Jacob Goldsmith, Esq.

Easton, Pa.—Moses Stern, Esq.

Harrisburg, Pa.—William Wolf, Esq.

Meadville, Pa.—Jacob Miller, Esq.

Baltimore, Md.—M. R. Walter, Esq.

Frederick, Md.—Henry Goldenberg, Esq.

Cumberland, Md.—Sieg. Rosenheim, Esq.

Hagarstown, Md.—D. Einstein, Esq.

Washington, D. C.—A. S. Solomon, Esq.

Georgetown, D. C.—B. Sinsheimer, Esq.

Richmond, Va.—Hon. William Lowenstein.

Norfolk, Va.—Rev. S. Mendelsohn.

Wheeling, Va.—Henry Frank, Esq.

Alexandria, Va.—Rev. A. A. Bonheim.

Petersburg, Va.—Rev. Alex. Gross.

Lynchburg, Va.—Max Guggenheimer, Jr., Esq.

Charlestown, W. Va.—Samuel Strauss, Esq.

Wilmington, N. C.—Solomon Beer, Esq.

Charleston, S. C.—Philip Wineman, Esq.

Savannah, Ga.—Jos. Rosenheim, Esq.

Columbus, Ga.—Rev. Bonheim.

Hon. Vice-Presidents—Continued.

Macon, Ga.—Jacob Harris, Esq.

Atlanta, Ga.—Rev. H. Gersoni.

Albany, Ga.—Hon. Ansel Sterne.

Augusta, Ga.—Rev. Lewinson.

Mobile, Ala.—I. I. Jones, Esq.

" " Rev. Dr. Moses.

Selma, Ala.—Jos. Myers, Esq.

Montgomery, Ala.—Rev. Jacobs.

Eufala, Ala.—Hy. Bernstein, Esq.

Vicksburg, Miss.—Rev. B. H. Gotthelf.

Natchez, Miss.—Isaac Lowenburg, Esq.

New Orleans, La.—Rev. J. K. Gutheim.

Shreveport, La.—J. A. Bergman, Esq.

Bayou Sara, La.—Major Simon Weil.

Clinton, La.—Joseph Israel, Esq.

Alexandria, La.—Julius Lewin, Esq.

Opelousas, La.—Emanuel Phillips, Esq.

Galveston, Tex.—Rev. A. Blum.

Houston, Tex.—Hy. S. Fox, Esq.

Columbus, Tex.—Hon. Hy. Merseburger.

San Antonio, Tex.—B. Oppenheimer, Esq.

Memphis, Tenn.—A. H. Frankland, Esq.

Knoxville, Tenn.—B. Burger, Esq.

Chattanooga, Tenn.—F. Decker, Esq.

Pine Bluffs, Ark.—Rev. Dr. M. Fluegel.

Little Rock, Ark.—Rev. Block.

Louisville, Ky.—Rev. Dr. Kleeberg.

St. Louis, Mo.—Isidor Bush, Esq.

St. Joseph, Mo.—Rev. S. Gerstmann.

Kansas City, Mo.—Jas. Kohn, Esq.

Cincinnati, O.—Lewis Seasongood, Esq.

Cleveland, O.—Rev. Dr. A. Hahn.

Youngtown, O.—E. Gutman, Esq.

Piqua, O.—H. Flesh, Esq.

Columbus, O.—J. Gundersheimer, Esq.

Hamilton, O.—Samuel Levy, Esq.

Portsmouth, O.—H. Richman, Esq.

Akron, O.—Isaac Cohen, Esq.

Dayton, O.—Rev. Fischer.

Fort Wayne, Ind.—Rev. Rubin.

Indianapolis, Ind.—Hon. Leon Kahn.

Evansville, Ind.—S. I. Lowenstein, Esq.

Wabash, Ind.—H. E. Sterne, Esq.

Vincennes, Ind.—S. Gimble, Esq.

La Fayette, Ind.—Isaac Baer, Esq.

Chicago, Ill.—Hy. Greenebaum, Esq.

Quincy, Ill.—Rev. Isaac Moses.

Milwaukee, Mich.—Rev. Dr. Spitz.

Grand Rapids, Mich.—Arthur C. Levi, Esq.

Detroit, Mich.—S. Heavenrich, Esq.

Beloit, Wis.—Chas. Newburgh, Esq.

St. Paul, Minn.—Rev. Dr. Winter.

San Francisco, Cal.—Alfred P. Elfeld, Esq.

Los Angelos, Cal.—Rev. Edelman.

Denver, Cal.—A. Jacobs, Esq.

Montreal, Canada East.—Rev. Dr. de Sola.

Toronto, Ont.—Samuel Solomon, Esq.

A FULL LIST OF MEMBERS WILL ACCOMPANY THE NEXT ISSUE.